From Numbers to Words

From Numbers to Words

Reporting Statistical Results for the Social Sciences

Susan E. Morgan
Rutgers University

Tom Reichert
University of Alabama

Tyler R. Harrison
Kean University

Allyn and Bacon

Boston ■ London ■ Toronto ■ Sydney ■ Tokyo ■ Singapore

Series Editor: Molly Taylor
Editorial Assistant: Sarah McGaughey
Marketing Manager: Jackie Aaron
Editorial-Production Service: Omegatype Typography, Inc.
Composition and Prepress Buyer: Linda Cox
Manufacturing Buyer: Julie McNeill
Cover Administrator: Kristina Mose-Libon
Electronic Composition: Omegatype Typography, Inc.

Copyright © 2002 by Allyn & Bacon
A Pearson Education Company
75 Arlington St.
Boston, MA 02116

Internet: www.ablongman.com

Library of Congress Cataloging-in-Publication Data

Morgan, Susan E.
    From numbers to words : reporting statistical results for the social sciences / Susan E. Morgan, Tom Reichert, Tyler R. Harrison.
        p. cm.
    Includes bibliographical references and index.
    ISBN 0-8013-3280-X (alk. paper)
    1. Social sciences—Statistical methods. 2. Statistics. I. Reichert, Tom. II. Harrison, Tyler R.   III. Title.

HA29 .M83165 2002
300'.7'27—dc21

                                                                2001018839

Printed in the United States of America

10   9   8   7   6   5   4   3   2   06   05   04   03   02   01

CONTENTS

PREFACE

There aren't many authors who are eager to have their own book published so that it will be available for their own use. When we were in graduate school, the three of us searched for a text like the one before you; unfortunately, such a book did not yet exist. We amassed a pool of examples to help us present the results of our work for our classes, for conference papers, and for publications, prizing those examples that were well written and complete. Because so many of our examples inconsistently reported elements of the analysis, we often had to do further research with various statistics texts. Once this research was complete, we found that we were using our own past work as the best example of what to do with our current research write-ups.

Of course, this book goes well beyond what we prepared for ourselves in graduate school. To complete this text, we scoured more than 5,000 additional empirical studies across several disciplines in the social sciences to find examples of well-written results. In it, you will find examples generated from such disciplines as psychology, communication, journalism, public health and health communication, mass communication, political science, sociology, as well as law and ethics.

This book will be an important supplemental text for anyone enrolled in an advanced undergraduate statistics class or a graduate class in methods or statistics. Moreover, it will be indispensable to anyone writing a master's thesis or doctoral dissertation based on an empirical study, as well as to the countless others writing papers for classes or for state, regional, national, or international conferences. For each test statistic we cover, we offer a format for how to write up the results of an analysis using that statistic, and follow this suggested format with one or more examples of how these tests have been written up for publication in the social sciences. These recent examples were chosen for their completeness, clarity, and readability, and we hope that they may even serve to model to readers how these statistics can be used appropriately in real-life research.

In contrast with those books that provide invaluable information about theories, ideas, and paradigms, our book is strictly a how-to guide. This is not a statistics text (although it is designed to supplement statistics texts) and is not intended to be a reference or a guide for which statistics to run for the analysis of a set of data. Rather, this book is meant to pick up where statistics books leave off. Once a student or scholar has the numbers representing the results of his or her labor, this book offers guidance for how to present these numbers in text and visual form. Consequently, we believe that this book will provide invaluable assistance to scholars of all levels as they seek to present and disseminate the results of their research. Furthermore, we believe that this book will prove to be an important guide to writing up results in the social sciences, and we hope that it will result in more consistent reporting of results across disciplines.

Acknowledgments

No project of this kind is possible without the help and support of many people. We would like to thank our editors at Addison-Wesley-Longman for their initial support of the book. Many thanks go to Karon Bowers at Allyn and Bacon for seeing the book through to fruition.

We would like to thank the following reviewers: Walid Afifi, Pennsylvania State University; Edd Applegate, Middle Tennessee State University; Robert Bostrom, University of Kentucky; Kay Colley, North Texas University; James Harwood, University of Kansas; Orayb Najjar, Northern Illinois University; Christopher Ogbondah, University of Northern Iowa; Michael D. Slater, Colorado State University; Wayne Wanta, University of Oregon; Stanley T. Wearden, Kent State University. They contributed greatly to the shape and scope of this book. Their attention to detail was invaluable. We appreciate also their enthusiasm for the idea behind this project.

Our statistics consultant, Craig Henderson, devoted a great deal of time to help us create an accurate as well as useful book.

We would be remiss without thanking Robert Bostrom for his encouragement and enthusiastic support for the project. We are also indebted to Sally Jackson, who believed that we could expand on a statistics independent study project (completed while we were graduate students) to create this book.

We would also like to thank our family members for being kind enough to act impressed that we were writing a book. They inspire us more than they know.

From Numbers to Words

.

1 How to Use This Book

Even scholars who entered the social sciences with the knowledge that they would have to become astute in the use of statistics have had to wrestle with the issue of how to present the results of their research. After struggling to learn statistical programs, such as SAS, SPSS, or Minitab (among others), and finally receiving the prized, newly analyzed data, many researchers must now confront the puzzling task of how to write up the results of their hard work. Even after scholars interpret the results of a statistical analysis, they must still make these results comprehensible to others. These others may include reviewers for journals or academic conferences, colleagues who are interested in the researcher's work, or (if these scholars are also students) their professors. Those who are interested in the statistical results of research need certain pieces of information so that they can obtain a clear picture of the data that have been collected. A well-written results section also will give readers clear answers to the hypotheses or research questions that were advanced prior to the collection of the data.

Unfortunately, it is very difficult to know how to write up the results of statistical analyses. Very little work has been done in this area, and even less is easy to use. An occasional textbook offers a few examples of a results section using a featured statistic, but it is usually unclear exactly what is required for a complete, well-written results section.

What This Book Is . . . and Is Not

The objective of this manual is to provide clear guidelines and examples for reporting the results of statistical analyses. In the following pages, we cover what information to present in a results section, including the statistical information needed for commonly used statistics, and the format for presenting this information through the use of examples. However, this is *not* a statistics textbook. As such, it will not help you decide what statistical procedures to use to analyze your data nor how to interpret the results you receive from those analyses. The following examples will, however, give you some clear guidelines for what to report in a results section and possible formats for the presentation of these results.

Because this book is the first of its kind, there has been little agreement on what should be included or how elements such as significance level should be reported. Therefore, you will note that a number of the examples deviate from some of our recommendations. Generally, these differences are not of central importance; some authors or editors may report that "$p < .0005$" instead of simply "$p < .001$," but this does not alter the meaning or usefulness of the report. This book offers a complete list of all elements for each statistical test that needs to be reported in a results section. The examples that follow each list are designed to demonstrate how all of those numbers can be strung together with words to create a coherent report. Whenever the examples lack a necessary element, we have provided information about what else should have been included. Because clear standards for reporting results have not been adhered to, complete examples for all statistics from the existing literature are remarkably difficult to come by. We sincerely hope that we have achieved a balance of information that will lead to complete and accurate reporting with real-life examples of the statistics in action.

Overview of the Book

We have divided this book into several sections. First, in Chapter 2 we provide an overview of the elements that you will need to include in your results section. We cover some basic and not-so-basic issues, such as reporting the effect sizes of your findings and the reliabilities of the instruments you use, as well as manipulation checks. We also provide a reference chart on Greek symbols and tips on how to create them in Word and WordPerfect. In Chapter 3, we cover the reporting of descriptive statistics, including frequencies, percentages, means, and standard deviations. These are the basic elements of statistical reporting. In addition, we provide guidelines for incorporating written text with tables. Cronbach's alpha for interitem reliabilities and Cohen's kappa and Scott's pi for interrater reliabilities are covered in Chapter 4. Correlation and measures of association appear in Chapter 5. These include commonly used correlation statistics such as Pearson's *r*. In Chapter 6, we show how to report nonparametric statistics, including the ubiquitous chi-square family of statistics as well as rank tests, among others. Parametrics tests are covered in Chapter 7, and include both the basics, such as *t* tests and ANOVA, as well as more advanced procedures, such as trend analysis and logistic regression. Finally, we have included a chapter on how to present results visually (Chapter 8). Although we provide many examples of tables throughout the individual sections on many of the statistics, we have created a number of guidelines to help you construct clear and effective tables and figures. These guidelines are followed by a number of examples of different types of tables and figures.

What You Should Do if a Statistic of Interest Is Not Included

These chapters should help you report the results of many statistical analyses. However, if the statistic that you are using in your study does not appear in this book, you have a couple of options. First, if your statistic is closely related to one of those represented in this book, it is likely that the pattern of reporting will be very similar. Second, you may want to use this manual for some aspects of reporting (such as the section on presenting your results in a visual format) and then do a search of the literature for other studies that use a similar statistic. Be sure to compare the results section that you locate with the information provided in Chapter 2 (the overview of conventional elements included in a results section), because journals may vary in terms of what elements or style they require.

2 Frequently Asked Questions about Reporting Statistics

"Results should be the payoff, the bottom line, the climax of the research report"

—(Shontz, 1986, p. 61).

Writing a good results section is not always simply an issue of formatting statistical results and choosing the right words. We've compiled a list of issues revisited frequently by most researchers, whether they are students or scholars. Some of these issues are basic whereas others are more advanced. These issues include

- What is a research report?
- What is a results section?
- What should I include in a results section?
- What are developing trends in reporting results?
- What is a manipulation check and how should I report it?
- How should I report the results of the tests of my hypotheses?
- What *exactly* should I report in my results section?
- What format should I use to report significance levels (*p* value)?
- What if my test is not significant?
- *Are* or *were* my results significant?
- What is an effect size (ES) indicator?
- Do I have to report the effect size?
- How do I report effect size?

- How do I use Greek symbols?
- Should I use tables?
- If I use tables, where do I put them?

As you use this book, you will notice that some of these issues are addressed in other chapters in more detail. However, this chapter should provide a brief overview of most of the important issues in constructing a solid results section.

What Is a Research Report?

Those new to the research process sometimes complain that journal articles are boring, no fun to read, and hence, deserving of their small readership. However, research reports aren't written to be appealing to the masses. Although entertainment is not a primary goal of journals within the social science domain, the straightforward communication of information is. Simply put, the primary purpose of journal articles is the dissemination of knowledge. Knowledge, according to mass communication researchers Stempel and Westley (1989), "can progress only as rapidly and as effectively as we can communicate our findings" (p. 388). It is, they say, the journal article, convention paper, or book that is the conduit for bringing new ideas and introducing significant findings into the field. Therefore, the transmission of information is vital to progress and is especially important to those who may benefit from research.

The communication of knowledge, via research reports, is purposely constructed with several goals in mind. First, reports are written so that the logic, method, procedure, and analysis of the project are open to inspection. Skepticism and critical judgment are highly valued in science. The constant questioning and detailed inquiry of research may seem overdone by people not familiar to the process, but it is only by this method that knowledge in our respective fields is advanced. Similarly, research must be replicable. Providing the opportunity for other researchers to replicate the study to confirm the conclusions and assumptions is another important value of science. For this reason, readers must be provided with the necessary detail to replicate the procedures and variables under study via the research report.

Research reports convey information in a specialized way. For example, most reports are organized in a sequential format that contains, in this order, a statement of the problem (review of literature and hypotheses), method, results, and conclusion. Because the outlets for this knowledge (i.e., journals) are limited, as is journal space, the report must communicate these elements as efficiently as possible. This means utilizing certain conventions and employing an economy of words with precise meaning. This allows readers of research to be able to dissect the report and access pertinent information quickly. The outline and style of writing are illustrative of the systematization of the scientific approach.

What Is a Results Section?

An important component of a methodological report is the results section. Results, as the section is typically labeled, contains a description of the results of statistical analyses as they relate to the hypotheses and research questions in the study. A primary goal of this section, according to the American Psychological Association manual (1994), is the summarization of data collected and the statistical treatment of that data. Williams (1979) defines the results component of the report more generally as a precise statement of the knowledge gained in the study. Suffice it to say, the results section is the portion of the report devoted to summarizing the data and describing the outcomes of various analytical procedures applied to that data.

What Should I Include in a Results Section?

There are certain types of information typically found in the results section. This section, as mentioned earlier, is stylized, which means it should be written according to a template common to research reports. Remember that some researchers may seek this information out first if they are interested in the analysis plan or the strength and/or magnitude of the findings. The results section is generally guided by the statements of hypotheses generated in the first part of the research report. As such, certain types of information should be included in a quantitative research report. However, because not every study has the same goals, you will have to decide what is most appropriate to include. Understanding the basic elements contained in a results section should be helpful. These include

- Manipulation checks
- Results of hypothesis testing
- Results summarized in tables and figures (typically placed at the end of your report)

What Are Developing Trends in Reporting Results?

Although they are not currently reported on a consistent or frequent basis, tests related to statistical assumptions and information that permits meta-analysis are two areas that are gaining attention in statistical reporting. These include

- Tests of assumptions (e.g., homogeneity, interdependence)
- Zero-order correlation matrix

Tests of assumptions provide the readers of research reports assurances that the statistical procedures being reported are appropriate given the nature of the data. Examples containing the report of these assumptions are very difficult to find in the published literature, but we recommend the reporting of these statistics. These tests include homogeneity of variance, normality, outliers, and others. We don't list these tests in individual chapters because editors appear not to demand it, so authors rarely report it, which means there are very few examples that model format or content. Nevertheless, we believe the trend is moving toward the reporting of this information because it gives both author and audience a more complete picture of the characteristics of the sample and helps readers assess the validity of the findings.

Additionally, given the increase in meta-analytic techniques, authors should include certain bits of information so that their studies may be included as part of a review of "knowledge." Certain pieces of statistical information related to a study's results are necessary for that investigation to be included as part of a meta-analysis. These bits of information include zero-order matrices among all variables and a restatement of dependent and independent variables used in the study. A zero-order matrix with reliabilities running in the diagonal, and mean and standard deviation in separate columns, would look like Table 2.1.

What Is a Manipulation Check and How Should I Report It?

In experimental research, many studies begin a discussion of results with a brief section describing the manipulation check. This is where you would report that your experimental manipulation worked as intended. For instance, when you say that you contrasted high versus low variables, how do you know that is how your research participants perceived them? You will want to offer evidence that the variables you may have manipulated were actually understood by receivers the way they were meant to be. The manipulation check is simply a check to determine whether the independent variable worked the way it was intended—or the levels of the independent variable behaved as expected.

Following is a simple example of a manipulation check used in a study to test two different types of crisis (e.g., accidents and

TABLE 2.1   Zero-Order Matrix

Variable	Mean	SD	A	B	C	D
A	7.00	.45	.84			
B	2.00	.32	.11	.90		
C	3.33	.11	.34	.22	.98	
D	5.00	.24	.10	.08	.28	.84

transgressions). The format is a good one to follow when you report your manipulation check.

> To assess the effectiveness of the experimental manipulations, a series of one-way analyses of variance (ANOVAs) were performed. To assess perceptions of crisis type, accidents and transgressions were compared on an item assessing perceptions of the organization's intentionality, $F(1, 275) = 27.78, p < .0001$. As expected, significant differences were observed, with participants rating transgressions as more intentional and accidents as less preventable. (Coombs & Holladay, 1996, p. 289)

How Should I Report the Results of the Tests of My Hypotheses?

The hypotheses and research questions set forth earlier in the report should be handled in sequential order, with a clear statement for each hypothesis as to whether it was accepted or rejected. Reminding yourself of what you were looking for may be a productive first step to writing up your results section. Sometimes a significant lapse of time between the construction of research questions or hypotheses and the analysis of the data can cause some initial confusion. Simply restating the hypotheses or research questions can be helpful in redirecting your efforts when reporting results.

You will want to remind your audience of your hypotheses as well. You can do this by rewriting your initial expectations and then stating what you found, supporting this with your numerical findings. For example:

> Hypothesis 1 predicted that reproach types would significantly differ from each other in their degree of perceived face threat. To test this hypothesis, mean levels of perceived face threats were compared across groups representing the four reproach categories. ANOVA indicated support for the hypothesis, $F(3, 87) = 53.79$, $p < .001, \eta^2 = .65$. (Carson & Cupach, 2000, p. 226)

Generally, the hypothesis is restated and followed by a statement that briefly describes the statistical analysis performed and outcome of that analysis. This would include a statement describing the test employed, the calculated statistic obtained (degrees of freedom and the value of test), and whether the outcome was significant. It is important to remember at this stage only to describe the results and not to draw conclusions. Similarly, one should abstain from claiming that a theory was supported or not supported at this stage, because theoretical support is dependent on several factors beyond the simple hypothesis test. It is vital to describe all relevant results so that readers can get a clear picture of the findings. This means that all findings, including those that run counter to the hypotheses, are reported.

Following is a simple, yet clear, example of a hypothesis test that is easy to follow and communicates all the necessary information:

> Hypothesis 1 predicted that concrete metaphors would be easier to understand than abstract metaphors. The results of a paired samples t test support this prediction, $t(102) = -4.43, p < .001, \eta^2 = .16$. Participants were more accurate in their interpretation of concrete metaphors ($M = 2.45, SD = .20$) than abstract metaphors ($M = 2.26, SD = .29$). (Morgan & Reichert, 1999, p. 6)

Note how the example contains all of the important elements appropriate for this type of test.

What *Exactly* Should I Report in My Results Section?

You will want to include the following elements for each hypothesis test when appropriate (see previous example).

1. *Restate the hypothesis or research question.* Reiterating this information will remind your reader of relevant variables and proposed relationships involving those variables. For example, in the first sentence of the previous example, the reader is reminded that the hypothesis predicted an advantage in comprehension for concrete metaphors.

2. *Identify the analysis and test statistic.* In this example, the test was identified as a "paired samples t test." If the analysis you report is somewhat controversial or violates important assumptions (e.g., using a *t* test to analyze ordinal level data), you will need to provide a brief explanation or justification. If you specify in advance a directional hypothesis, indicate that after reporting the effect size [e.g., t (102) = –4.43, p < .001, η^2 = .16, one-tailed]. Nondirectional tests (two-tailed) are assumed in the social sciences. If you use a two-tailed test, you do not need to identify it as such.

   3. *Identify the value of the test statistic, degrees of freedom, p value, and effect size.* The observed value of the test statistic is essential to report, in combination with a report of effect size and significance level. Although alpha levels of .05 and .01 are very common in the social sciences, it is recommended in the APA manual (1994) that you explicitly state the alpha level used for your tests. If you set a different alpha level, you need to provide a brief justification. (See the following discussion of this issue.)

   4. *Provide a conclusive statement of the result.* The magnitude of the test statistic may not always provide enough information for readers to discern whether the values you are reporting are in the direction you predicted. Therefore, it is helpful to accompany your report of the statistic with a brief translation of whether the result supports your hypothesis. In the previous example, the reader is reminded that the result offers support for the hypothesis.

   5. *Include descriptive information* (e.g., means and standard deviation). The most basic information about your results is often the most useful. This information often appears in accompanying tables when there are too many conditions to report efficiently in the text of a results section. Descriptive statistics reported in a results section usually include measures of central tendency (e.g., means, medians) and variance (e.g., standard deviation). Most of the chapters in this text recommend that you offer information about the proportions or means of the groups being compared. Information about the means gives the reader an easy way to pinpoint the values being compared. Even if the results obtained were not significant, information about the means can still help the reader get a sense of the difference between groups.

   6. *Other information specific to the type of test may need to be included.* The syntax in the previous example provides guidelines of what typically appears in the report of a simple hypothesis test. Other information that may need to be reported will vary from statistic to statistic. For this reason, it is important to consult the chapter that corresponds to the test you are conducting. If the test you are performing is not represented in this text, consult a well-respected journal in your field that publishes similar research.

What Format Should I Use to Report Significance Levels (p Value)?

An important part of the analysis process is the determination of alpha and levels of significance in your studies. As such, significance levels are important components that need to be incorporated into your reports.

In most disciplines within the social sciences, alpha is typically set at .05 or .01. If a different level is used, the researcher should provide brief justification. Regardless, APA recommends that you state your alpha level either in a general statement (e.g., "An alpha level of .05 was used for all statistical analyses") or with each test.

Significance levels can be reported in one of two ways. You may use signs to indicate the general probability of having obtained this statistical value by chance (e.g., $p < .05$, $p < .01$, $p < .001$), or you may report exact levels ($p = .028$). Depending on the style of the journal to which you are submitting a manuscript, or the organization or university to which you belong, or even your own personal style, you may want to report exact significance levels (p values). Some readers prefer to know the exact value of p so that they can assess for themselves whether to pursue further research in this topic. In addition, readers may have different ideas regarding where alpha should be set. If an exact value is reported, these readers can more easily determine if the null hypothesis would have been rejected given a more conservative alpha level. For the purposes of this book, we recommend reporting the exact p value. Whatever you decide, it is important to note that p cannot equal zero. For example, some junior researchers mistakenly report $p = .000$ because this value appears on the printout. In this situation, report $p < .001$.

You will need to decide whether to report the exact value of *p* or simply to indicate whether your results reached the level of significance you aimed for. If the results are nonsignificant (you fail to reject the null hypothesis), you can indicate this by giving the results of the statistic followed by the letters *ns*, or you could report $p > .05$ or $p > .10$. Another option is to report the exact significance level (e.g., $p = .13$).

What if My Test Is Not Significant?

It is common for a study to produce statistically nonsignificant findings for one or all tests of hypotheses or research questions. Although you may feel compelled to cover up or brush aside results that fail to support your hypotheses, you must report them. According to the APA manual, you should report all relevant results, even if the results are contrary to what you expected. For example, if the *t* test reported earlier was not significant, we might report it this way: "Hypothesis one predicted that concrete metaphors would be easier to understand than abstract metaphors. The results of a paired samples *t* test failed to support this prediction, $t (102) = -.43, p > .10$." Always remember that good science is transparent, not deceptive.

Are or *Were* My Results Significant?

You should use the past tense to describe your results when you report them in the results section of your paper. For instance, you might state, "Communication apprehension was related to familiarity with the topic," or "Evaluations increased significantly." On the other hand, use the present tense when discussing the results and presenting conclusions in the discussion section.

What Is an Effect Size (ES) Indicator?

Often researchers and practitioners are concerned with determining how much influence the experimental manipulation had on participant responses. In medical research, for instance, researchers would likely want to know more than if the effect of different dosage levels was significant at the .05 level or the .01 level. They would also want to know if the dosage differences had any meaningful impact on the patient's health. Measures of effect size, like other descriptive statistics, provide us with that information.

Effect size is generally thought of as the magnitude of an experimental effect. Rosenthal and Rosnow (1984, p. 22) define it as the degree to which the observed relationship differs from zero. Others have described effect size as a measure of the strength of the relationship of interest (Jaccard & Becker, 1997). These indices are important because they allow researchers to make judgments about whether an observed finding is trivial or substantive. In addition, knowing effect size can assist us in designing more powerful experiments by helping us determine appropriate sample size. Effect size is also helpful to researchers conducting meta-analyses because these indicators enable the comparison of findings across studies.

There are two general types of effect size indicators. Those that compare differences between treatment means are referred to as standardized mean differences. Common indicators of this type include Cohen's d, Hedges's g, and Glass's Δ (point biserial correlation). The other type of effect size is based on measures of association (correlation and explained variance). Correlational indicators include Pearson's r, Spearman's r_S, point biserial r_{pb}, and ϕ (phi coefficient), among others (Fern & Monroe, 1996). Indicators that account for the amount of variance in the dependent variable accounted for by the independent variables include η^2 (eta-squared), ω^2 (omega-squared), ε^2 (epsilon-squared), partial ω^2, and ρ_I (intraclass correlation coefficient) (ANOVA designs). For regression designs, indicators include r^2, semipartial r^2, and R^2. The APA manual (1994, p. 18) provides a list of other common effect size indicators.

Rosnow and Rosenthal (1996) suggest that Cohen's d, Hedges's g, and Pearson's r are the most relevant and widely acceptable effect size indicators. If you are unfamiliar with effect size, we recommend you refer to Fern and Monro (1996) and Richardson (1996), as well as other references cited in this section, for a discussion of statistical properties and advantages and disadvantages of various effect sizes indices.

Do I Have to Report the Effect Size?

Because not every report of a statistical study contains effect size information, you may be wondering whether you should include it. We suggest that effect size information, along with the results of the statistical analysis (e.g., F value), be included in your report. Others have made similar recommendations (Cohen, 1965; Hays, 1963; Jaccard & Becker, 1997; Richardson, 1996; Rosenthal, 1991). In addition, the fourth edition of the APA manual encourages researchers to provide effect size information in their reports.

There are three important reasons for including effect size indicators in your report. The first has to do with what Chow (1988) calls the substantive-significance problem of significance tests. Chow and others have argued that there has been an overreliance on the statistical test for interpreting the meaningfulness and practicality of an effect. Rosnow and Rosenthal (1996) go further by stating that researchers tend to "obsess" on p values. Researchers rely on the heuristic that a significant p value implies an effect of important magnitude. In reality, the magnitude of an association or the magnitude of the influence of one variable on another may be trivial. We don't mean to imply, however, that null hypothesis testing is inappropriate. Cortina and Dunlap (1997) argue that there are many cases in which drawing conclusions about hypotheses based on p value is reasonable. Suffice it to say that reliance on a p value or effect size alone is controversial. Reporting p values and effect sizes helps others evaluate the meaningfulness of observed effects independent of the level of statistical significance.

The second important reason for reporting effect size is that researchers can use the information provided in your study to conduct better research. Reported effect size can be helpful when planning research because it, along with sample size, determines the power of an experiment. Researchers can look to studies like yours in the literature to gauge the range of published effect sizes for the phenomena of interest. This will help them decide how many respondents they need for their own research in order to test their hypotheses adequately. In addition, with the emergence of meta-analysis, it has become more important for researchers to be able to glean the effect sizes reported in studies easily.

Third, reporting effect size increases the accessibility of your study to a wider audience. Although relatively simple procedures have been developed to determine effect sizes from the information provided in your report of statistical tests (means, cell sizes, test values, etc.; see Rosnow & Rosenthal, 1996), not everyone is conversant in these procedures. Researchers should strive to ensure their results are accessible to a wide spectrum of research consumers, including practitioners, graduate students, and scholars in fields less conversant with statistical analyses and procedures. Keep this in mind: Readers of research are not necessarily doers of research. Although journal space is inherently limited, a brief statement of effect size is worthy of inclusion in your report.

How Do I Report Effect Size?

The effect size indicator you choose to report should be clearly linked to a corresponding test of significance. There are two general ways to report effect size.

   1. Include effect size in the syntax for the corresponding statistical test. Although authors vary where they place it in the enumeration, we recommend that it be reported immediately after the p value.

R-squared
The factorial MANOVA for the handgun topic indicated main effects for inoculation condition, $F(8, 716) = 3.07, p < .01, R^2 = .03$, and involvement, $F(8, 716) = 3.28, p < .001, R^2 = .04$. (Pfau, Tusing, et al., 1997, p. 199)
   Results indicated a significant relationship, $R = .39, F(1, 58) = 10.58, p < .002, R^2 = .15$, thereby supporting this study's second hypothesis. (Seiter, 1997, p. 244)

Eta-squared
A significant effect emerged for relational type in Story 1, $F(1, 492) = 7.33, p < .007, \eta^2 = .01$, in which typical story readers

were rated as less aware about justifying secondary goals (Story 1: $M = 2.74$) than when reading about personal involvement in a developing romance (Story 1: $M = 2.96$). (Honeycutt, Cantrill, Kelly, & Lambkin, 1998, p. 56)

Omega-squared
Results revealed a significant interaction effect, $F(1, 81) = 39.78$, $\omega^2 = .33, p < .0001$, which explained 33% of the variance (see Figure 3). (Leets & Giles, 1997, p. 287)

Phi coefficient
Results indicated a significant relationship ($\phi = .86$, $\chi^2 = 40.27$, $df = 1$, $p < .001$), thereby supporting the first hypothesis of this study. (Seiter, 1997, p. 243)

Cramer's V
A log-linear analysis on the percentage of children who perceived that the main character felt negative resulted in a significant main effect for inclusion of subplot, $G^2 (N = 148) = 7.39, p < .01, V = .04$. (Weiss & Wilson, 1998, p. 597)

2. Write a short descriptive sentence about the nature of the effect. If you choose to report your effect size in this manner, be sure it follows immediately after the reported significance test. Examples of brief descriptive statements include the following:

Also, the relationship between type of humor and type of program was strong (Cramer's $V = .80$). (Potter & Warren, 1998, p. 50)

This difference was statistically significant, as indexed by the Humor 1c Program interaction, [. . .] the degree of association was [. . .] Cramer's $V = .32$. (Potter & Warren, 1998, p. 51)

Whichever method you use to report effect size, always include the appropriate effect size indicator and its associated value. If the indicator is signified with a Greek letter (e.g., γ, ε, η, Δ), and the letter is available on your word processor, type the letter in the appropriate place and do not underline it in your manuscript. If you don't have Greek letters on your word processor, either handwrite the symbol or type the name of the indicator (e.g., eta-squared, gamma, delta). Otherwise, underline all other statistical symbols (e.g., $\underline{r}$, $\underline{d}$, $\underline{V}$).

How Do I Use Greek Symbols?

Greek symbols are essential to reporting the results of statistical analyses. When you use them, Greek symbols should not be underlined or italicized. If you use a word processor, Greek symbols can easily be incorporated into your report.

Microsoft Word

If you use Microsoft Word, select INSERT from the toolbar. Then select SYMBOL from the drop-down menu. Alternatively, from the FONT drop-down menu, select SYMBOL. Simply choose the lowercase Greek letter that reflects the test or effect size indicator used in your study. To superscript a number or letter, highlight it and use the [Control + Shift + =] keys. This will allow you to create the notation for a chi-square (χ^2), eta-squared (η^2), or other symbols requiring a superscript.

WordPerfect

In WordPerfect, use the [Control + W] keys. In the CHARACTER SET menu, select GREEK. To create a superscript, highlight the text you wish to change, press [F9], and select superscript under the POSITION menu.

According to the APA manual (1994), you are also permitted to write in the symbols for Greek-notated statistics manually. An advantage of placing the Greek symbol in your manuscript with your word processor is that you have a permanent record of your results on your computer; you will not have to remember what was in the blank spot in your manuscript.

Some commonly used Greek symbols are listed in Table 2.2. Abbreviations for other statistical tests not covered in this text can be found in fourth edition of the APA manual (1994) on page 115.

TABLE 2.2   Greek Symbols

Greek Letter	What It Is	Definition
α	Alpha	Probability of Type I error; Cronbach's index of internal consistency
β	Beta	Probability of Type II error; $(1 - \beta)$ is statistical power; standardized multiple regression coefficient
γ	Gamma	Goodman-Kruskal's index of relationship
Δ	Delta (cap)	Increment of change
η^2	Eta-squared	Measure of strength of relationship
Θ	Theta (cap)	Roy's multivariate criterion
λ	Lambda	Goodman-Kruskal's measure of predictability
Λ	Lambda (cap)	Wilk's multivariate criterion
ν	Nu	Degrees of freedom
ρ	Rho (with subscript)	Intraclass correlation coefficient
Σ	Sigma (cap)	Sum or summation
τ	Tau	Kendall's rank correlation coefficient; also Hotelling's multivariate trace criterion
φ	Phi	Measure of association for a contingency table; also a parameter used in determining sample size or statistical power
ϕ^2	Phi-squared	Proportion of variance accounted for in a 2×2 contingency table
χ^2	Chi-squared	Computed value of a chi-square test
ψ	Psi	A statistical comparison
ω^2	Omega-squared	Measure of strength of a relationship
^	Caret	When above a Greek letter (or parameter), indicates an estimate (or statistic)

Should I Use Tables?

It is important to report the data in sufficient detail to both justify the conclusions and allow inspection of the data. An economical way to do so is by summarizing the data in tables. Depending on the size and complexity of the study, the descriptive information can be provided in the text or in a table. If provided with descriptive statistics (mean, standard deviation) and the test statistic, it's relatively simple for researchers to piece together important information about the data. Tables should visually communicate and simplify the data, but tables should be used sparingly. A table should not simply repeat what is reported in the text but should expand upon or clarify what is in the table. On the other hand, tables should present only those data that are relevant to the hypotheses. Tables serve an important function, but, as always, remember to limit the number of tables to what is absolutely necessary. Consult Chapter 8 on visual communication for additional tips on constructing effective tables, charts, and figures.

If I Use Tables, Where Do I Put Them?

Place tables at the end of your report, just after the reference section. Place only one table on a page and number them. According to the latest version of APA style, you are no longer required to specify table placement within the text. Simply refer to the appropriate table, beginning with Table 1. You must refer to every table you use. You might say, " . . . as indicated in Table 2," or "(see Table 2)." Last, tables, as well as the entire manuscript, should be double-spaced.

Conclusion

Reporting the results of your research should strike a balance between providing the necessary technical information and making yourself clear to your intended audience. You may find that you are writing for an audience that is unfamiliar with statistics. In that case, a well-written results section should provide a naive reader with information necessary for interpreting the importance of your findings. In addition, effectively presenting the results of statistical analyses will lend credibility to your assertions, especially when critical members of your audience *are* knowledgeable.

It seems most productive to assume that your audience has a basic but limited understanding of statistics, although APA recommends you assume your reader has a professional knowledge of statistics. Either way, you can provide the necessary information for a motivated person to investigate your results further, while being clear and simple enough so that your report is complete. Remember, good ideas presented clearly are more powerful than good ideas presented in a needlessly complicated or obscure fashion.

This book is designed to help you report your results succinctly and accurately according to commonly accepted conventions. The following chapters are designed to demystify the process of reporting the results of your analyses. We hope that the principles and examples offered will result in better and more complete reports of your statistical analyses. There is, however, no substitute for good writing. Shontz (1986) provides some excellent advice regarding the principle of balance in your writing: "The ideal report contains the maximum possible amount of the most necessary information in the least possible space" (p. 54).

3 Descriptive Information

Descriptive statistics help to summarize data that have been collected and/or manipulated in a study. These statistics range from the simple reporting of group membership (e.g., political party affiliation) to measures of central tendency and variance.

Frequencies and percentages often provide simple nominal level data. Data are typically described in two ways. One involves measures of central tendency (e.g., mean, median, mode), and the other is more closely related to the distribution or dispersion of scores (e.g., variance, range, standard deviation, percentages). Means and variance are used not only to summarize characteristics of data but also to estimate relationships among variables within the population. As such, descriptive statistics are important to include in the report of your results because they provide meaningful information to the reader.

TOPICS INCLUDED IN THIS SECTION:

Frequencies and Percentages   Mean and Standard Deviation

Frequencies and Percentages

What to Report
- Size of overall data set (N)
- Size of a cell or group (n)
- Percentages (%)

Suggested Format   ■ Respondents were recruited from
communication courses ($N = 65$).

■ Males represented a smaller proportion
of the sample ($n = 25$) than women
($n = 40$).

■ Of those participating in the study, only
35% were aware of the manipulation.

Note: In every study involving respondents or counts, the size of
the data set must be reported. Typically, this information is lo-
cated in the section that describes the method of the study. In
some cases, it may be appropriate to report it in the results section. Regarding percentages, you should use the percentage sign
(%) in the text only if a numeral is placed before it. Otherwise, use
the word *percentage*.

Examples from the Literature

In the following example, the authors describe the results of their
survey about adolescent drug solicitation as both frequencies (n)
and percentages (%).

> Seventh-grade participants who were offered drugs were asked to
> describe the physical location of the offer. Most drug offers oc-
> curred in *public places* such as school, on the street, or at a park
> (43%; $n = 36$); at their own or a friend's *home* (28%; $n = 23$); or at a
> *social setting* such as a party (7%; $n = 6$). (Hecht, Trost, Bator, &
> MacKinnon, 1997, p. 84)

Leach and Braithwaite (1996) provide a standard account of
information about the sample in their study. As is common, they
report information about their respondents in terms of the percentage of the sample.

> Three hundred and fourteen respondents completed the survey in-
> strument, 179 males (59%) and 134 females (43%). The respon-
> dents' ages ranged from 17–50, with a mean of 21 years. The
> majority of respondents were Anglo-American (76.4%), followed
> by Hispanic-Americans (13.69%), African-Americans (5.09%),

Asian-Americans (1.9%), and Native-Americans (1.59%). (Leach & Braithwaite, 1996, p. 204)

The following table reports the percentage of birth control stories in the *New York Times* from 1915 to 1917 (Flamiano, 1998, p. 562). Tables can be an effective way to describe nominal data. See Chapter 8 to see how to visually communicate your results or refer to Table 3.1.

Mean and Standard Deviation

What to Report   ■ Mean (*M*)
                     ■ Dispersion measure (*SD*)

Suggested Format ■ The mean of group one (*M* = 3.25, *SD* = 1.12) was greater than that of group two (*M* = 2.45; *SD* = .99).

Examples from the Literature

The following report uses means, standard deviations, and percentages to describe the sample. The total number of observations was reported elsewhere in the article.

In this study, for the cross-sectional sample, children are defined as those 19 years or younger. The average age of children during the

TABLE 3.1 *New York Times* Birth Control Coverage, by Topic

Year	N	Legal Issues	Advocates	Opponents	Neutral
1915	7	—	86%	14%	—
1916	28	68%	14%	7%	11%
1917	39	74%	15%	3%	8%
Total	74	65%	22%	5%	8%

Note. From "The Birth of a Notion: Media Coverage of Contraception, 1915–1917," by D. Flamiano, 1998, *Journalism and Mass Communication Quarterly, 75* (3), p. 562.

three cross-sectional waves was 15.2 years (SD = 2.15) at baseline, 14.9 years (SD = 2.06) during intervention, and 14.7 years (SD = 2.22) at follow-up. Of the sample, 51% at baseline, 46% during intervention, and 45% at follow-up were girls. (Rimal & Flora, 1998, p. 617)

Descriptive statistics are frequently reported in tables. Table 3.2 contains all the necessary information as well as percentages when describing career barriers toward female news anchors (Engstrom & Ferri, 1998, p. 794).

TABLE 3.2   Perceived Career Barriers for Women Television News Anchors

Description of Item	N	Mean	SD	Strongly Agree/ Agree	Neither Agree nor Disagree	Disagree/ Strongly Disagree
Overemphasis on Physical Appearance	128	3.86	1.14	75%	7%	18%
Conflicts between Roles of Wife/Mother and Newscaster	122	3.64	1.20	62%	20%	18%
Balancing Family and Job	128	3.52	1.16	63%	11%	26%
Lack of Professional Network	127	3.42	1.02	53%	27%	20%
Having to Relocate	128	3.38	1.24	54%	19%	27%

Note. (1) The greater an item's mean, the greater its importance as a career barrier. (2) Percentages may not equal 100 due to rounding and missing values. From "From Barriers to Challenges: Career Perceptions of Women TV News Anchors," by E. Engstrom & A. J. Ferri, 1998, *Journalism and Mass Communication Quarterly, 75* (4), p. 794.

4 Reliabilities

Reliabilities come in various shapes and sizes, and although they are typically reported in the method section, it is important to be familiar with common usage. Three commonly reported reliability indicators are Cronbach's alpha coefficient, Cohen's kappa, and Scott's pi. In this chapter, we provide a description of each indicator and provide examples of how you can report each test.

TESTS INCLUDED IN THIS SECTION:

Interitem Reliability
  Cronbach's Alpha

Interrater Reliability
  Cohen's Kappa and Scott's Pi

Interitem Reliability

Cronbach's Alpha

What to Report   ■ Observed reliability coefficient (α or Cronbach's alpha)

Supporting information (reported in text or table)
   ■ Descriptive statistics (M and SD)

Suggested Syntax   ■ $\alpha = .80$
   ■ Cronbach's alpha = .80

Suggested Format   ■ Reliability was acceptable (α = .80).
                     ■ Cronbach's alpha was .80.

Note: Cronbach's alpha, also referred to as alpha coefficient and coefficient alpha, is a measure of internal consistency and is typically found in the description of the materials used in your study. Aside from reporting the coefficient only, it is also important to provide a description of the measures (including means and standard deviations) used to derive reliability.

Examples from the Literature

In the following example, note the manner in which the authors report a series of interitem reliabilities accompanied by appropriate descriptive statistics. Although they include the recommended information in their write-up, more detailed information on the nature of each subscale appears elsewhere in the article.

> We averaged responses within each subscale resulting in measures of *the perceived acceptability of socializing* (α = .80, M = 5.92, SD = 1.08), *the perceived acceptability of dating* (α = .88, M = 3. 81, SD = 1.83), *the frequency of socializing* (α = .77, M = 5.04, SD = 1.09), and *the frequency of dating* (α = .82, M = 2.18, SD = 1.22). (Solomon & Williams, 1997, p. 205)

The next example employed instruments from previous research. Note how the authors include the means and standard deviations from their study as well as a comparison to previously published uses of the instruments.

> Cronbach alphas for SMS Extraversion, Acting, and Other-Directed subscales were .65, .72, and .65, indicating that the scales had acceptable internal consistency. Scale means were 10.44 (SD = 5.24) for PMR, 3.62 (SD = 1.73) for SMS Extraversion, 2.31 (SD = 1.68) for SMS Acting, and 3.44 (SD = 2.11) for SMS Other-Directed. The means, standard deviations, and alphas are comparable to those obtained in previous studies (see Briggs et al., 1980; Rest, 1975). (Rotenberg, Hewlett, & Siegwart, 1998, p. 170)

Interrater Reliability

Cohen's Kappa and Scott's Pi

What to Report
- Observed reliability coefficient (κ or Cohen's kappa/π or Scott's pi)
- Percentage of agreement
- Number of items coded to establish reliability
- Number of coders

Suggested Syntax
- $\kappa = .80$
- Cohen's kappa = .80
- $\pi = .80$
- Scott's pi = .80

Suggested Format
- Interrater reliability on the 20 items was acceptable as indexed by Cohen's kappa ($\kappa = .85$). The percentage of agreement between the two independent coders was 89.9%.
- Cohen's kappa was .80.

Examples from the Literature

Cohen's Kappa   Interrater or intercoder reliability measures the internal consistency of raters/judges/coders in applying a scale of measurement. The most common test for interrater reliability with categorical data is Cohen's kappa, which corrects for chance agreement. In this example, percentage of agreement is not provided. Reporting this information is helpful to readers of your report.

> [A]ll three authors independently coded the remaining 8 scripts from the pilot study. We computed a Cohen's Kappa coefficient to assess the reliability of these codings by computing word by word across each pair of coders (Keppel, 1982). This analysis yielded a Kappa coefficient of .74. . . . We held back 10 scripts for another

reliability check midway through our coding, which yielded a Kappa coefficient of .84. (Morrill, Johnson, & Harrison, 1998, pp. 652–653)

In the following example, the researchers describe a multi-stage coding process in addition to reporting intercoder reliability. Rather than reassessing validity at the midpoint, the authors selected random scripts at the end of the process. Note the reporting of percentage of agreement in this report, as well as kappa.

At the beginning of the coding process, four transcripts were randomly selected and separately coded to estimate intercoder reliability. Intercoder agreement was 75.1% for the six categories, and Cohen's (1960) kappa was acceptable ($\kappa = .67$). Disagreements in coding use were then discussed and resolved. To provide an index of coder drift, four transcripts coded at the end of the process were randomly selected and independently coded by the same two researchers. Surprisingly, percent of agreement and Cohen's kappa increased (89.9% agreement; $\kappa = .85$). (Canary, Brossman, Brossman, & Weger, 1995, pp. 194–195).

Scott's Pi   In the following example, another form of interrater reliability, Scott's pi, is reported. Note that the authors did not report the number of items used to establish reliability.

Reliability was measured both by percentage agreement and Scott's pi (Holsti, 1969). The latter measure adjusts the reliability estimate to account for agreement expected by chance. Reliability estimates were high—message type: agreement = 92%, Scott's pi = .88. (Hummert, Shaner, Garstka, & Henry, 1998, p. 134)

CHAPTER

5 Correlation

The two most commonly reported correlation techniques are covered in this chapter: Spearman rank-order correlation and Pearson product-moment correlation. If you plan to construct and report a correlation matrix, refer to Chapter 8.

TESTS INCLUDED IN THIS SECTION:

Correlation
Spearman Rank-Order Correlation
Pearson Product-Moment Correlation

Correlation

Spearman Rank-Order Correlation

What to Report	■ Degrees of freedom (df)
	■ Observed r_s value (r_s)
	■ Significance level (p)
Suggested Syntax	■ r_s (df) = observed r_s value, significance level
Suggested Format	■ As hypothesized, there was a significant correlation between the groups, r_s (24) = .39, $p < .01$.

Note: The rank-order correlation is also referred to as Spearman's rho and rank correlation coefficient. Reporting effect size is not necessary because it can easily be obtained by squaring the observed r_s value. Spearman rank-order correlation is reported several ways depending on the style of the journal and the discipline. The suggested format example is clear for the reader and contains the necessary information. A correlation matrix can be constructed and reported in the text as a table (refer to Chapter 8 on creating effective tables).

Examples from the Literature

Here follows an example of a Spearman rank-order correlation reported in the literature. Please note that degrees of freedom, group ranks, and sample size are reported in a table (not shown). These researchers refer to the test as Spearman rho. Although not included in this example, reporting the degrees of freedom and/or sample size is important in your write-up. Note that variance accounted for is the same as the observed rank-order value squared.

> The ranked, self-reported news values of the two groups (SEJ vs. SEPR—see Table 1) was a strong (Spearman rho) rank-order correlation of $r_s = .86$ ($p < .01$), accounting for 74% of the variance. (Sallot, Steinfatt, & Salwen, 1998, p. 370)

Not all analyses yield significant results. The next example reports a Spearman rank-order correlation in which two comparisons were not significant. Note that n was reported instead of degrees of freedom and that a two-tailed test was used. Typically, only directional tests are identified.

> There was no correlation in the data set between discussion size and either the proportion of contributions in pairwise conversations overall or the proportion of contributions in long conversations (Spearman $r_s = 0.26$ and 0.08, respectively, $n = 21$, ns). However, discussion size was correlated with the proportion of new floor contexts (Spearman $r_s = .61$, $n = 21$, $p < .005$ two-tailed). (Carletta, Garrod, & Fraser-Krauss, 1998, p. 542)

Pearson Product-Moment Correlation

What to Report
- Observed r value (r)
- Significance level (p)
- Degrees of freedom   (df)

Supporting information
(reported in text or table)
- Descriptive statistics (M and SD)

Suggested Syntax
- r (df) = observed r value, significance level

Suggested Format
- As hypothesized, there was a significant correlation between the groups, r (24) = .39, $p < .01$.

Note: Pearson is similar to Spearman's rank-order correlation in terms of reporting test results. Although the reader can determine which correlation you ran by looking at your description of measures, be sure to indicate which test was run to avoid confusion.

Examples from the Literature

This brief report by Cozzarelli and Karafa (1998) of the positive correlation between two items of interest contains all the necessary information for reporting a correlation.

> The participants indicated their agreement with these items using 7-point Likert-type scales ranging from 1 (strongly disagree) to 7 (strongly agree). The two items were positively correlated, $r(154) = .76, p < .001$. (Cozzarelli & Karafa, 1998, p. 260)

In the following example, the researcher describes the results of several correlation analyses. Note that all three correlations were negative. Descriptive statistics are reported elsewhere in the article.

The hypotheses were tested through the computation of the correlation between the CFQ and (a) the IIS, (b) the Revised Self-Monitoring Scale, and (c) the RCQ. Because the CFQ is a measure of cognitive failure, higher scores indicate lower levels of cognitive efficiency.

H1. The first hypothesis was supported. The CFQ was significantly related to the interaction involvement scores, $r(145) = -.52$ ($p < .01$). The CFQ exhibited significant negative relationships with all three internal factors of the IIS, CFQ and attentiveness: $r(145) = -.54$, $p < .01$; CFQ and perceptiveness: $r(145) = -.36, p < .01$; CFQ and responsiveness: $r(145) = -.45, p < .01$. (Jordan, 1998, p. 12)

Partial Correlation　Following is an example of a report that distinguishes between zero-order and partial correlations. Note that the author did not report degrees of freedom in this section of the report. You should include it in your report.

Both simple and partial correlational techniques found a significant relationship between private self-consciousness and the domains of Openness (zero-order $r = .40$, $p < .001$; partial $r = .39$, $p < .001$) and Agreeableness (zero-order $r = -.23$, $p < .05$; partial $r = -.19, p < .05$). (Scandell, 1998, pp. 585–586)

CHAPTER

6 Nonparametric Statistics

Nonparametric statistics are frequently used in the social sciences to examine the differences or associations for nominal and ordinal level data. You may notice that the number of elements you should include in the report of your study is often considerably less than what is required when you write up the results of parametric tests. However, especially in the case of chi-square tests, the text of a results section is very often accompanied by a table. We have provided examples of how to integrate both text and tables in this chapter.

You will also notice that effect sizes are rarely stated in the results reports of nonparametric statistics. However, this is not because such measures do not exist; it simply appears that this has become a convention in published research. We recommend that you include effect sizes in your report. If you would like models of how to incorporate the report of effect sizes in your results section, please consult the discussion regarding effect size in Chapter 2. If you need to review nonparametric statistics, *Nonparametric Statistics for the Behavioral Sciences* by Siegel and Castellan (1988) is an excellent resource.

TESTS INCLUDED IN THIS SECTION:

Chi-Square Tests

Wilcoxon Rank Sum Test/ Mann-Whitney *U* Test

Kruskal-Wallis Test

McNemar's Repeated Measures Chi-Square Test for Change

Cochran's *Q*

Wilcoxon Signed-Rank Test

Friedman Analysis of Variance by Ranks Test

Chi-Square Tests

What to Report
- Degrees of freedom (df)
- Number of observations (N)
- Observed chi-square value (χ^2)
- Significance level (p)
- Effect size (ES, varies with test)

*Supporting information
(reported in text or table)*
- Number of observations per cell (n)
- Table of frequencies/percentages (optional)

Suggested Syntax
- χ^2 (df, N = XX) = observed chi-square value, significance level, ES

Suggested Format
- A 2 × 3 chi-square test indicated that the relationship between gender and promotion was significant, χ^2 (2, N = 112) = 13.45, $p < .01$, $V = .29$.

Note: The suggested syntax is similar for chi-square tests. This includes goodness-of-fit test, Fisher's exact test, and other chi-square tests. Briefly identifying the type of test is essential (e.g., "a Fisher's exact test revealed" or "a chi-square goodness-of-fit test indicated"). Frequencies and percentages can be reported within the text and/or a table. Tables are recommended, however, because they enhance reader comprehension.

Examples from the Literature

Goodness-of-Fit Test: The chi-square goodness-of-fit test, also referred to as a single sample chi-square test, determines whether frequencies across categories of a variable are distributed in relative manner. The following is a good example because the authors briefly remind the reader of the hypothesis, variables, and statistical test used to test the relationship. Note that all necessary information, except effect size, is contained in this example.

Consistent with the second hypothesis, a significant majority of participants used two or more temporally linked causes to form at least one chain. A chi-square goodness of fit test showed that the number of participants who chained, $n = 61$ (68%), was significantly greater than those who did not, $n = 28$ (32%), $\chi^2(1, N = 89) = 12.24$, $p < .0005$. (Gold & Shaw, 1998, p. 658)

In the following example, Brashers and Jackson (1999) reported a chi-square test with an appropriate effect size. Note that N and degrees of freedom were not reported in the syntax but were reported in a table referred to by the authors.

> The issue of whether to include replications affects research in a very wide range of subfields. By our coding, 35% of all articles ever published in *HCR* reported studies in which replications were (arguably) needed. Of these, 58% actually incorporated replications into the design. However, the proportion is not homogeneous throughout the 24-year publishing history. Instead, among studies published before Volume 9, only 46% used replications, whereas for those published after Volume 9, 63% did so ($\chi^2 = 5.23$, $p < .05$, $\phi = .16$).[2] These proportions fluctuate considerably from year to year; Table 1 and Figure 1 provide a summary of proportions from each of the eight completed editorships. (Brashers & Jackson, 1999, pp. 460–461)

If you use Yates's correction for continuity, you should report it. In the following example, the researchers report that Yates's correction and Fisher's exact test were employed when appropriate, but that these tests yielded essentially the same values as a goodness-of-fit chi-square test. The researchers also refer the reader to a table listing descriptive information. Note that in this example, effect size was not reported. You are strongly encouraged to report the effect size.

> For each city, goodness-of-fit (chi-square) analyses, with and without Yates' correction, as well as Fisher's Exact Test, were performed on the data concerning frequencies of positive and negative responses. In each case, the degree of association between the frequency of positive and negative responses concerning room availability, and inclusion or exclusion of the homosexual reference, was examined. Results using Yates' correction, and Fisher's

Exact Test, yielded essentially the same results and p-levels as those reported below.

Table 1 [not included here] shows frequencies of positive and negative responses for the individual and pooled samples.

Use of the homosexual reference significantly affected the proportion of positive and negative responses concerning availability; for Windsor, $\chi^2(1, N = 60) = 8.29$, $p < .004$; for London, $\chi^2(1, N = 60) = 11.92$, $p < .001$; for Detroit, $\chi^2(1, N = 60) = 19.46$, $p < .001$. For the three cities' data pooled together, $\chi^2(1, N = 180) = 23.32$, $p < .0001$. No differences according to gender of caller (Table 1), or of landlord, were found. (Page, 1998, p. 34)

Fisher's Exact Test   Fisher's exact test is an alternative to a traditional chi-square when expected frequencies are small. Generally, the Fisher test approximates chi-square distribution as N increases. The following example is supported by Table 6.1, in which the result of the statistical analysis is reported. This is a common practice in some journals. However, it is recommended that you report the appropriate statistical summary in the text (e.g., degrees of freedom, test value, and effect size) to aid readability.

Contrary to Ansolabehere and Iyengar's (1995) strongly expressed conclusion that attack ads depress turnout least among Republicans, Republicans turned out less often when exposed to Gordon Smith's attack ads (see Table [6.1]). (Lemert, Wanta, & Lee, 1999, pp. 128–129)

Two/K Sample Chi-Square Test   The following is an example of a 2×4 chi-square test. The relationship between artist gender and clothing type was tested in a content analysis of country music videos and found to be significant. The researchers highlighted several important percentages in the text, but placed most information in Table 6.2. Reporting the effect size would have made the report of this chi-square analysis complete.

Alluring clothing appeared in six female artists' videos (7.5%) and usually consisted of wet t-shirts, lingerie, or men's tailored shirts with apparently nothing on underneath. Male country artists typically wore blue jeans and long-sleeved Western shirts. Ten of the

TABLE 6.1   Turnout Rates among Republicans by Reported Exposure to Type of Smith Ad

Did Vote?	Yes	No	Total
Positive/mixed ad[a]	93%	7%	100% ($N = 14$)
Negative ad	58%	42%	100% ($N = 26$)

Note. Turnout records from county election department. [a]Three of these 14 cases said the ad was both positive and negative, $p < .05$, two-tailed Fisher's exact probability test. From "Party Identification and Negative Advertising in a U.S. Senate Election," by J. B. Lemert, W. Wanta, & T. T. Lee, 1999, *Journal of Communication, 49* (2), p. 128. Used by permission of Oxford University Press.

male artists' videos (4.9%) included somewhat alluring clothing (i.e., skintight leather pants or transparent shirts). The relationship between artist gender and clothing type was significant, $\chi^2(3, N = 282) = 57.17, p < .001$. (Andsager & Roe, 1999, pp. 77–78)

TABLE 6.2   Clothing Allure by Artist Gender

	Clothing Type				
Artist Gender	Neutral ($n = 236$)	Somewhat Alluring ($n = 37$)	Alluring ($n = 7$)	Implied Nudity ($n = 2$)	Total
Female ($n = 80$)					
Row	57.5%	33.7%	7.5%	1.3%	100%
Column	19.5%	73.0%	85.7%	50.0%	
Male ($n = 202$)					
Row	94.1%	4.9%	0.5%	0.5%	100%
Column	80.5%	27.0%	14.3%	50.0%	
Total	100%	100%	100%	100%	

Note. $\chi^2(3, N = 282) = 57.17, p < .001$. From "Country Music Video in Country's Year of the Woman," by J. L. Andsager & K. Roe, 1999, *Journal of Communication, 49*, p. 78. Used by permission of Oxford University Press.

The following report comes from a study examining self-reports of tomboyism by at least three categories of age cohort. The researcher provides a succinct description of the results following the report of the statistical outcome. The statistical syntax was placed within parentheses, which may have been the style for this particular journal.

Sixty-seven percent of the sample ($N = 315$) described themselves as tomboys during their childhoods with 32% of them describing the behavior as occurring "most" of the time. Table 1 displays responses to the central questions about tomboyism by age cohort. Chi-square analyses revealed a significant difference among the generations ($\chi^2(2, N = 463) = 32.73, p < .001$). Seniors were less likely to report being tomboys than were the two younger cohorts. When age was considered as a continuous variable, the strength of the relationship between age and the dichotomous tomboy behavior variable (yes/no) was small with $\eta = .30$, with eta representing the strength of association between a nominal and interval variable, ($\eta^2 = .09$). (Morgan, 1998, pp. 793–794)

Wilcoxon Rank Sum Test/ Mann-Whitney U Test

What to Report
- Observed z or U value (z/U)
- Significance level (p)
- Effect size (ES, varies with test)

Supporting information
(reported in text or table)
- Number of observations (N)
- Number of observations per group (n)
- Mean ranks

Suggested Syntax
- Group 1 ($n = $ XX) was significantly different from Group 2 ($n = $ XX), z [or U] = observed z [or U] value, significance level, ES.

Suggested Format ■ The Wilcoxon rank sum test revealed that Group A ($n = 35$) was less likely to spend time watching television than Group B ($n = 35$), $z = 1.28$, $p < .01$, $r_g = .23$.

Note: A z is reported for the Wilcoxon test. It is also reported for the Mann-Whitney test (instead of U), if one of the sampled groups is larger than 20. As always, be sure to clearly identify which test you report (e.g., "a Mann-Whitney U test indicated" or "a Wilcoxon rank sum test"). Number of observations and mean ranks can be reported in the text or a table. Although effect sizes are rarely reported for these tests, we strongly recommend that they be included to aid interpretability. The findings can be summarized within the text and/or a table.

Examples from the Literature

The following example of a Wilcoxon rank sum test contains all the necessary information except N and group size, which were reported in an accompanying table. Note that effect size in the form of the Glass rank biserial coefficient was reported in this example.

> Controlling for sex of the model, a Wilcoxon rank sum test was applied to the ranked data. For an alpha level of .05, the mean ranks between year and female dress (454.20 for 1983; 513.89 for 1993) were significantly different, $z = -3.96$, $p < .001$. The strength of the relationship, as indexed by the Glass rank biserial coefficient, was .12. Women were more likely to be dressed in a sexually explicit manner in 1993 compared to 1983. (Reichert, Lambiase, Morgan, Carstarphen, & Zavoina, 1999, p. 11)

In the following report, the z (lowercase) was reported for the Mann-Whitney U, as well as mean ranks and sample size. As previously noted, z was used because at least one of the groups had over 20 respondents. Once again, we recommend stating the effect size in your report.

Mann-Whitney U analyses revealed significant differences between volunteers and direct mail members in their rankings of the goals of storm drain pollution prevention and sewage treatment. As proposed, the sum of the average ranks that volunteers assigned to the dominant goal of storm drain pollution prevention was significantly higher (M rank = 88.78, $n = 59$) than the sum of the average ranks assigned by direct mail members (M rank = 57.18, $n = 81$) $z(140) = -4.67, p < .0001$. (Collins-Jarvis, 1997, p. 11)

Kruskal-Wallis Test

What to Report
- Degrees of freedom (df)
- Number of observations (N)
- Observed test value (H or χ^2)
- Significance level (p)
- Effect size (ES, varies with test)

Supporting information
(reported in text or table)
- Number of observations per group (n)
- Mean ranks

Suggested Syntax
- H (df, N = XX) = observed H value, significance level, ES

Suggested Format
- The Kruskal-Wallis test indicated a significant effect, H (2, $N = 25$) = 12.47, $p < .01, \eta^2 = .07$.

Note: The format for reporting Kruskal-Wallis test results is similar to the one for reporting results of the chi-square test. For this test, H is reported unless there are more than three groups or the sample size for one group is greater than five. If these conditions are violated, χ^2 is reported. Also, remember to indicate that you used a Kruskal-Wallis test (e.g., "a Kruskal-Wallis analysis of variance indicated . . ."). The findings can be summarized in the text and/or within a table.

Example from the Literature

This simple example illustrates that reporting a Kruskal-Wallis test doesn't have to be long to contain an almost complete statistical summary. Effect size is not reported in this example, but it is important for you to include it in your report. In addition, please note that χ^2 is reported instead of H, which suggests that either more than three groups or at least one group having more than five members was used in the study.

> A Kruskal-Wallis analysis of variance (ANOVA) revealed that accuracy varied significantly across communication conditions, $\chi^2(2) = 12.89$, $p < .01$. (Graetz, Boyle, Kimble, Thompson, & Garloch, 1998, p. 730)

McNemar's Repeated Measures Chi-Square Test for Change

What to Report
- Degrees of freedom (df)
- Number of observations (N)
- Observed chi-square value (χ^2)
- Significance level (p)
- Effect size (ES, varies with test)

Supporting information
(reported in text or table)
- Number of observations per cell (n)

Suggested Syntax
- χ^2 (df, N = XX) = observed chi-square value, significance level, ES

Suggested Format
- A McNemar test indicated a significant effect, χ^2 (2, N = 112) = 13.45, $p < .01$, $V = .29$.

Note: The McNemar test uses a syntax similar to that for a chi-square test. As always, be sure to identify the type of test (e.g., "A

McNemar test was conducted . . ."). The findings can be summarized in the text and/or within a table.

Example from the Literature

The following example reports the results of two nonsignificant analyses using the McNemar test. In addition, note that sample size (N) and degrees of freedom were included within the statistical statement, but because the results were nonsignificant, the example lacks a statement of the effect size.

> McNemar's repeated measures chi-square test for change did not indicate any significant difference from using either the latency measures, χ^2 (1, N = 121) = 2.00, p = .16, or the Edwards scale χ^2 (1, N = 121) = .69, p = .41, by themselves. (Holden, 1998, p. 393)

Cochran's Q

What to Report
- Degrees of freedom (df)
- Number of observations (N)
- Value of test statistic (Q or χ^2)
- Significance level (p)
- Effect size (ES, varies with test)

Supporting information
(reported in text or table)
- Number of observations per cell (n)

Suggested Syntax
- Q (df, N = XX) = observed test value, significance level, ES

Suggested Format
- The Cochran's Q test revealed a significant effect, Q (2, N = 78) = 12.38, p < .01, V = .09.

Example from the Literature

The following report by Pbert et al. (1999) weaves the results of several statistical analyses between the text and Table 6.3. The researchers restated the relationship they sought to examine and referred readers to the table for a summary of results. Sample size and effect size, not included below, are needed to make your report complete.

> To assess whether the three sets of data from patients, audiotape, and physicians differed significantly on individual intervention steps, Cochran's Q tests were computed. Table [6.3] presents the overall incidence of the observed presence of steps as reported by

TABLE 6.3 Comparison of Patient, Physician, and Audiotape Assessments on Frequency on Intervention Steps

Intervention Step	PT (%)	Tape (%)	MD (%)	Q^a
Discussed smoking	100	100	100	—
Advised to stop	89.8	71.3	100	29.3**
Discussed reasons	87.0	74.1	75.0	9.6*
Discussed past experiences	80.5	71.3	74.1	5.6
Discussed problems	83.3	75.9	65.7	13.0*
Discussed specific strategies	86.1	58.3	58.3	40.9**
Discussed dependency	56.5	54.6	60.2	1.4
Agreed to stop	54.6	35.2	40.7	20.6**
Agreed to cut down	20.4	8.3	16.7	9.5*
Set date to stop/cut down	36.1	14.8	21.3	30.9**
Put plan in writing	2.8	1.9	3.7	3.0
Discussed other changes	38.9	11.1	34.3	33.7**
Given written materials	34.3	31.5	35.2	3.3
Set follow-up visit	28.7	32.4	56.5	28.0**
Plan to discuss at future visit	43.5	12.0	14.8	37.3**

Note. PT = patient report; Tape = audiotape assessment; MD = physician report. Tabulated values are percentage of total encounters reporting completion of the specific step. From "The Patient Exit Interview as an Assessment of Physician-Delivered Smoking Intervention: A Validation Study," by L. Pbert et al., 1999, *Health Psychology, 18* (2), p. 186. Copyright © 1999 by the American Psychological Association. Reprinted with permission.

[a]Q is distributed approximately as χ^2 with 2 *dfs* testing the overall difference in percentage responding favorably in the three assessments.

*p < .01. **p < .0001.

each assessment source and the probability that these observations are dissimilar across sources. As the table indicates, significant differences between the patient report, audiotape assessment, and physician report were observed for 10 of the 15 intervention steps. (Pbert et al., 1999, pp. 185–186)

Wilcoxon Signed-Rank Test

What to Report
- Observed test value (T or z)
- Number of observations (N)
- Significance level (p)
- Effect size (ES, varies with test)

Supporting information
(reported in text or table)
- Rank sums (the number of $+/-$'s) (SS)
- Descriptive statistics (M and SD)

Suggested Syntax
- N = XX, T = observed test value, significance level, ES

Suggested Format
- A Wilcoxon signed-rank test revealed a significant difference in responsiveness between the first and second application, $N = 32$, $T = 12$, $p < .01$, $r_C = .23$.

Note: Also referred to as the Wilcoxon matched-pairs signed-ranks test, this test can be reported a number of ways. The Wilcoxon T is reported unless the number of matched pairs is larger than 25; if pairs are greater than 25, z is reported. Although effect size is rarely found in the published literature, it should be included in your report to aid interpretability. The findings can be summarized in the text and/or within a table.

Examples from the Literature

Grier and Firestone (1998) provide an example of a Wilcoxon signed-rank test with a z value instead of T because N is larger than 25. The researchers do not list degrees of freedom or effect size, which are both recommended. Other information can be found in the table to which they refer the reader (not shown). In addition, although they identified the test as nondirectional (two-tailed), only directional (one-tailed) tests are typically identified as such.

> Wilcoxon signed rank tests were also performed using these same dependent variables. The average positive and negative ranks for both groups are presented in Table 2. For efficacy, the treatment group advanced on means-end attributes with more children showing positive (M = 9.92, SS = 119) than negative (M = 6.80, SS = 34) ranks, z = 2.01, p < .05, two-tailed. (Grier & Firestone, 1998, pp. 278–279)

As with the previous example, z is reported instead of T in the next example. The authors provide a justification for using the Wilcoxon test and note their use of a Bonferroni correction. The following report incorporates information about the means and standard deviations into the text of the results section rather than using a table for this information. Note how the effect sizes are re-ported at the end of the paragraph. This is fine as long as you are sure to include the effect size indicator so readers are clear which one you employed. If you elect to present your results completely in text format, this would be a good model for reporting your findings as long as you include N and degrees of freedom as shown in the format example.

> A Wilcoxon matched-pairs signed-ranks test was performed on the data because nonparametric tests were believed to be the most ap-propriate form of analysis for this study due to the use of rank-ordered data. A Bonferroni correction was applied to the alpha levels to control for the possibility of a Type 1 error (because of the number of tests used). Participants tended to favor: females over males (z = 3.25, p < .01; Males: M = 8.64, SD = 4.53; Females: M = 8.32, SD = 4.69), nondrinkers opposed to drinkers (z = 13.38, p < .005; drinkers: M = 9.61, SD = 4.13; nondrinkers: M = 7.36, SD = 4.79), those with lower rather than higher incomes (z = 17.17, p < .005; high income: M = 10.07, SD = 4.32; low income: M = 6.89, SD = 4.33), and Christians over nonreligious patients (z = 9.85, p < .005; atheists/agnostics: M = 9.12, SD = 4.76; Christians:

$M = 7.85$, $SD = 4.36$). The effect sizes of the four variables are shown in Table 1 (.69 for income; .49 for alcohol consumption; .28 for religion; and .07 for gender). (Furnham, Meader, & McClelland, 1999, pp. 740–741)

Friedman Analysis of Variance by Ranks Test

What to Report
- Degrees of freedom (df)
- Number of observations (N)
- Observed χ_r^2 value (χ_r^2 or χ^2)
- Significance level (p)
- Effect size (ES, varies with test)

Supporting information (reported in text or table)
- Mean ranks
- Number of observations per cell (n)

Suggested Syntax
- χ_r^2 (df, N = XX) = observed test value, significance level, ES

Suggested Format
- A Friedman analysis of variance by ranks test indicated that a change in galvanic response differed across the three groups, χ_r^2 (2, N = 14) = 11.02, $p < .01$, $W = .14$.

Note: The report of Friedman analysis of variance by ranks uses a syntax similar to that for chi-square and Kruskal-Wallis tests. If the number of conditions is greater than 4 or n in any group is greater than 9, χ^2 is reported instead of χ_r^2. The effect size measure for the Friedman's test is the Concordance Coefficient W, which is seldom reported in the literature. It is recommended that you state effect size in your reports. The findings can be summarized in the text and/or within a table.

Example from the Literature

This study, an examination of the relationship between novices and specialists, contains all the elements necessary in a report of a statistical procedure for this particular analysis except effect size. Notice that chi-square (χ^2) is reported because there are more than four cells. Mean ranks and other descriptive information are reported in a table (not shown).

> Table 1 presents the median usefulness rank of each document in each group and for each problem. Using Friedman's chi-square test, we found a significant difference in the rankings of the documents both in the novice group, $\chi^2(6, N = 11) = 12.78, p < .05$, and $\chi^2(6, N = 11) = 17.81, p < .01$, and in the specialist group, $\chi^2(6, N = 8) = 34.84, p < .001$, and $\chi^2(6, N = 8) = 29.04, p < .001$, for Problems 1 and 2, respectively. (Rouet, Favart, Britt, & Perfetti, 1997, p. 92)

CHAPTER

7 Parametric Statistics

Parametric statistics differ in several ways from the nonparametric statistics reported in Chapter 6. Common parametric analyses—*t* tests, analysis of variance, and regression, among others—have assumptions such as a quantitative dependent variable measured in a way that at least approximates interval level. These tests also have different assumptions regarding distributions of scores within the population of interest. For these reasons, what needs to be included in the results section will differ to some degree from what is reported for nonparametric statistics.

Descriptive indicators provide important information that needs to be included in your report, such as measures of central tendency (e.g., mean, median, mode) and the distribution of scores (e.g., range, variance, standard deviation). Other standard features in a report of analyses using parametric statistics, especially tests of differences (*t* tests, ANOVA, MANOVA), include the test value, degrees of freedom, significance level, and effect size. Post hoc and planned comparisons are additional statistics that are commonly reported with these tests. Tests that examine relationships (e.g., correlation, regression) need to incorporate reports of measures of association such as R-squared, r, and beta-weights. Tables are particularly helpful for summarizing the results of statistical results as well as information about the descriptive statistics. Tabachnik and Fidell (1996 or latest edition) is an excellent resource if you need to refresh your knowledge of the multivariate statistics found in this section.

TESTS INCLUDED IN THIS SECTION:

z Test

t Test

Analysis of Variance (ANOVA)
  ANOVA with Interaction
    Effects
  Post Hoc Tests
  Planned Contrasts
  Trend Analysis
  Log Transformation and
    Trend Analysis

ANCOVA

**Multivariate Analysis of
Variance (MANOVA)**
  Manova with Bartlett's Test of
    Sphericity

MANCOVA

**Regression and Multiple
Regression**
  Stepwise Multiple Regression
  Hierarchical Multiple
    Regression

Logistic Regression

z Test

What to Report
- Degrees of freedom (df)
- Observed *z* value (*z*)
- Significance level (*p*)
- Effect size (ES, varies with test)

*Supporting information
(reported in text or table)*
- Number of observations (*N*)
- Sample mean and standard deviation
  (*M* and *SD*)

Suggested Syntax
- *z* (df) = observed *z* value, significance
  level, ES

Suggested Format
- The sample mean was different from the
  population mean, *z* (39) = 2.21, *p* < .01,
  η = .07.

Note: There are various uses of the *z* test. Be clear regarding which one you employ. Classically, when the population standard deviation is known, a *z* test is used rather than the *t* test. This occurs so infrequently, however, that *z* tests are rarely used or reported.

If you do have occasion to report one, use the suggested syntax format outlined.

Examples from the Literature

z **Test of Proportions**   A *z* test, a test of difference between proportions, is more commonly reported for frequency data. For this test, use the suggested syntax format outlined but replace descriptive statistics with frequencies and percentages. The following authors restate their hypotheses and describe the results of their statistical analyses. This example also demonstrates how to report nonsignificant findings. Please note that tables in the article report *n* sizes and proportions of characters by year and age.

> A total of 1,228 adult speaking characters were identified in the sample and 63% of those characters were male. Only 2.8% of the 1,228 characters were judged to be over 64 years of age.
> . . . Hypothesis one predicted that the proportion of characters over 65 would have increased since 1975. However, a test of the difference between two proportions indicated no support for this hypothesis ($z = .62, p > .54$). In fact, the percentage of characters over 65 decreases from 4.5% in 1975 to 2.8% in 1990.
> . . . Hypothesis three predicted that the proportion of female characters would have increased since 1975. . . . While the percentage of female characters 65 or older did increase slightly from 3.4% in 1975 to 4.4% in 1990, the test of the difference between two proportions indicated no support for this hypothesis ($z = 1.61$, $p > .11$). (Robinson & Skill, 1995, p. 115)

This brief but useful example includes the elements needed to report the results of a *z* test. The percentages that would normally appear in such a report are provided elsewhere in the article. The researchers included an effect size indicator (η) for the *z* test.

> The results indicated that the semantic cues and situation information were attended to by the subjects (situation: four of 146 were incorrectly recalled, $[z] = 11.83, p < .001, \eta = .98$; semantic cue: eight of 146 were incorrectly recalled, $[z] = 11.25, p < .001, \eta = .93$). (Grewal, Marmorstein, & Sharma, 1996, p. 151)

Note: In the original article, *z* was reported as *Z*.

t Test

What to Report   ■ Degrees of freedom (df)
■ Observed *t* value (*t*)
■ Significance level (*p*)
■ Effect size (ES, varies with test)

Supporting information
(reported in text or table)
■ Number of observations (*N*)
■ Number of observations per cell (*n*)
■ Descriptive statistics (*M* and *SD*)

Suggested Syntax   ■ *t* (df) = observed *t* value, significance level, ES

Suggested Format   ■ An independent groups *t* test revealed that Group 1 ($M = 2.45$, $SD = .49$) differed from Group 2 ($M = 2.29$, $SD = .45$) as predicted, t (df) = 3.98, $p < .01$, $\eta^2 = .05$.

Note: The syntax is similar for one-group, independent, and correlated groups *t* tests. For that reason, it is important to indicate clearly which test was conducted with a statement such as "a one-group *t* test revealed." Also report an appropriate effect size measure; common effect size measures associated with *t* tests include eta-squared and *d*.

Examples from the Literature

Independent Groups t Test   This example highlights the results of a *t* test to determine whether subordinates who behave in an assertive fashion receive fairer treatment than those who display low-assertiveness behavior. Note that *r* was reported as a measure of effect size. This is a well-written example of an independent groups *t* test because it contains all the necessary elements to easily interpret and corroborate the findings.

A *t* test was used to test the effects of the assertiveness manipulation on ratings of interactionally fair behavior, revealing a significant difference between conditions, $t(40) = 4.35$, $p < .05$; r ([between] condition, [and] interactionally fair behavior) = .57. On average, participants in the high-assertiveness condition displayed more interactionally fair behavior than did participants in the low-assertiveness condition (high assertiveness: $M = 2.31$, $SD = 0.49$; low assertiveness: $M = 1.51$, $SD = 0.65$). Thus, the hypothesis that assertive communication evokes higher levels of interactionally fair behavior was supported. However, it is noteworthy that the means in both conditions were quite low given that the scale ranged from 0 to 7. (Korsgaard, Roberson, & Rymph, 1998, pp. 734–735)

Correlated Groups t Test   This brief example from a study examining the effect of two different types of metaphors contains all of the elements necessary for a correlated group (also referred to as paired samples or paired comparison) *t* test, although the standard deviations appear in a table. Also note that the suggested syntax was enclosed within parentheses. This varies from APA guidelines but is common for journals in marketing. Always consult the style manual most commonly used in your discipline or the journal you will be submitting your article to for information on the precise format you should adopt. However, this difference in style does not affect the substance of what is reported.

Hypothesis 1 predicted that concrete metaphors would be easier to understand than abstract metaphors. The results of a two-tailed paired samples *t* test supported this hypothesis, $(t(102) = -4.43$, $p < .001$, $\eta^2 = .16$). Participants were more accurate in their interpretation of concrete metaphors ($M = 2.45$) than abstract metaphors ($M = 2.26$). (Morgan & Reichert, 1999, p. 6)

Analysis of Variance (ANOVA)

What to Report
- Degrees of freedom (between and within) (df_B / df_W)
- Observed F value (F)
- Significance level (p)
- Effect size (ES, varies with test)

*Supporting information
(reported in text or table)*
- Number of observations (*N*)
- Number of observations per cell (*n*)
- Descriptive statistics (*M* and *SD*)

Additional information for factorial designs
- Variable names
- Nature of design (within or between subjects)

Suggested Syntax
- F (df$_B$, df$_W$) = observed F value, significance level, ES

Suggested Format (example is of a factorial design)
- The means for each of the groups (shown in Table 1) indicated that influence of variable X on variable Y was in the direction predicted. The 2 (message directness) × 3 (message length) between groups ANOVA revealed that the hypothesis was supported, F (2, 63) = 12.47, $p < .01$, $\eta^2 = .17$.

Note: Reporting the results of F tests is fairly similar to the reporting of ANOVA test results (one-way, factorial between and within tests). Be sure to indicate clearly which type of test you are reporting so that it is clear to the reader. It is also strongly recommended that you include a measure of effect size, which can vary depending on the preference of the researcher and the type of ANOVA. A common effect size for analysis of variance is eta-squared, although R^2 and r are also reported in the examples that follow. We have included examples of one-way and factorial ANOVAs, as well as supplemental analyses such as post hoc tests, planned contrasts, and trend analysis. If you are unclear about the type of ANOVA you are running or the correct statistical procedures, please consult a statistical text.

Examples from the Literature

One-Way ANOVA   The use of a one-way analysis of variance (ANOVA) is illustrated in this study on compliance gaining by Roloff and Janiszewski (1989). Note that degrees of freedom are reported differently from the suggested syntax. As always, it is important to remember that disciplines, and even journals within disciplines, vary as to how the results of statistical tests are reported.

> To assess the adequacy of operationalized intimacy, two tests were performed. First, the relationship between the two measures of intimacy was examined. A one-way ANOVA indicated significant differences in communication intimacy across the three levels of manipulated intimacy ($F = 123.38$, $df = 2/117$, $p < .001$, $eta^2 = .68$). A higher level of intimate communication was reported in the friend condition ($M = 53.66$, $SD = 14.83$), followed by the acquaintance ($M = 30.53$, $SD = 10.13$) and stranger conditions ($M = 15.56$, $SD = 6.54$). (Roloff & Janiszewski, 1989, p. 47)

Factorial ANOVA   Factorial ANOVA merely reflects the fact that the analysis includes more than one independent variable. Those independent variables can be "between subjects" in nature, "within subjects/repeated measures" in nature, or have some combination therein. The report is similar to suggested syntax noted above except that main effects and interactions can be tested and subsequently reported. When reporting factorial ANOVAs, make sure to identify the independent variables and the nature of the variables (e.g., within or between subjects).

Between Groups ANOVA   This study examines the effect of making respondents aware of their own mortality on behavior toward people who violate social norms. This is a good example of how a standard factorial ANOVA can be presented. Notice that the researchers reported how many groups existed for each of the variables. That information can be communicated many ways as long as it is clear and easy to understand. Also note that both main effects were significant as well as the interaction between the two variables. Means and standard deviations were reported in a table.

A 2 (mortality salient vs. exam control) × 3 (feedback: social deviant vs. conformist vs. neutral) between-participants ANOVA on these social projection scores revealed a main effect for feedback, $F(2, 68) = 10.49$, $p < .001$, $R^2 = .24$, and a main effect for mortality salience, $F(1, 68) = 7.38$, $p < .01$, $R^2 = .10$. These main effects were qualified by the predicted Condition × Feedback interaction, $F(2, 68) = 36.00$, $p < .001$, $R^2 = .54$. Mean social projection scores for each group are presented in Table 1. (Simon et al., 1997, p. 1061)

The following example incorporates everything you need to report, except standard deviations, in order to make your results clear and complete. Note that no post hoc tests were reported because each variable (exposure/sex) had only two levels.

An analysis of variance was conducted on the ratings of how much children liked worms. The analysis resulted in a highly significant main effect for the live exposure component of desensitization, $F(1, 141) = 10.91$, $p = .001$, $\eta^2 = .07$. Children who were exposed to live earthworms in a modeling context reported that they liked worms more ($M = 4.7$) than did those who were not exposed to worms ($M = 3.4$). The only other significant finding was a main effect for sex, $F(1, 141) = 14.98$, $p < .001$, $\eta^2 = .10$. Boys liked worms ($M = 4.9$) more than did girls ($M = 3.2$). (Weiss, Imrich, & Wilson, 1993, p. 57)

Repeated Groups ANOVA   Notice how the following example begins with a restatement of the hypotheses being tested, the nature of the design (e.g., repeated measures), followed by a list of the variables that factored into the statistical test. In this example, the results are reported for only the first test. In addition, the authors' write-up includes the necessary elements, although the descriptive statistics (means and standard deviations) appear elsewhere in the article.

Our first hypothesis predicts that message explicitness is a dominant force shaping perceptions of harassment, while *H2* and *H3* suggest that message effects will be influenced by situational cues. To evaluate these predictions, we conducted a repeated measures ANOVA examining the effects of the within-subjects manipulations of initiator's power, initiator's sex, target's sex, initiator's attractiveness, target's attractiveness, and all interactions.

Results indicated that evaluations of messages as sexually harassing were overwhelmingly determined by message explicitness, $F(1, 78) = 693.27, p < .001, eta^2 = .88$. (Solomon & Williams, 1997, p. 205)

ANOVA with Interaction Effects

The following ANOVA presents the results of both main and interaction effects. Means and effect size are presented in table format in the article but are not included here. Note how the author clearly states the variables being tested in the interaction, and interprets the interaction with a descriptive sentence interpreting the simple effects.

Evaluations were subjected to the Hero Humor Involvement (absent, present) × Villain Humor Involvement (absent, present) × Respondent Gender (male, female) analysis of variance. The analysis of Distress yielded a significant main effect of gender $F(1, 148) = 44.63, p < .001$, with male respondents reporting less distress ($M = 3.07$) than did female respondents ($M = 5.67$). An interaction between hero humor involvement and gender, $F(1, 148) = 3.40, p < .050$, also was found. Analysis of the simple effects of hero humor revealed that women found the film significantly more distressing when hero humor was present, whereas men found the film marginally less distressing when hero humor was present. Significant interactions between hero humor and gender were also found for the single item distress measure, "How distressed did this video clip make you feel?," $F(1, 152) = 5.05, p < .026$, and evaluations of the violence as distressing (as queried by the single adjective scale), $F(1, 152) = 7.21, p < .008$ (see Table 1). (King, 2000, pp. 16–17)

Post Hoc Tests

If your overall F test is significant, you may want to report the results of a post hoc test. Three common tests include the student Neuman Kuels, Tukey, and Scheffe (reported in the following). Which one to report is a judgment call as all three have their strengths and weaknesses. You should refer to a reference source to determine which is preferable given the context. If standard deviations aren't reported in a table, you should include them in the text.

> To examine H3, H4, and H5, organizational image was analyzed using a 2 (crisis type: accident vs. transgression) × 2 (crisis occurrence: one-time vs. multiple) × 3 (organizational response type: no response vs. matched response vs. mismatched response) ANOVA. As expected, the results revealed significant main effects for crisis type, $F(1, 230) = 28.59, p < .0001, \eta^2 = .12$, performance history, $F(1, 230) = 59.61, p < .0001, \eta^2 = .21$, and response type, $F(2, 230) = 9.06, p < .0001, \eta^2 = .07$. Table 4 [not shown] summarizes the ANOVA results. To assess pairwise differences among the three levels for the main effect for response type, the Scheffe follow-up procedure ($p = .05$) was performed. The results indicated that image assessments for the matched response ($M = 3.15$) differed significantly from both the no-response ($M = 2.63$) and the mismatched response ($M = 2.63$). H3, H4, and H5 were supported by the findings. (Coombs & Holladay, 1996, p. 292)

Planned Contrasts

The example below is from a study that examines the suppression of racial stereotypes. The paragraph provides an excellent description of their use of contrast tests. Note that planned contrasts sometimes use a t value instead of the usual F test, but they are still part of an ANOVA design. Whether you use a t or an F (most common) will depend on the way your contrasts are executed. Although effect size isn't included in this example, it's strongly recommended that you state effect size in your reports.

> Planned contrasts were then conducted in order to test our hypothesis that participants in both the directed suppression and the spontaneous suppression conditions would make more stereotypic ratings than participants in the control conditions. Consistent with this prediction, participants in the directed suppression ($M = 7.92, SD = .98$) and the spontaneous suppression ($M = 7.80, SD = 1.15$) conditions rated Donald as significantly more hostile (i.e., in a manner more consistent with the African-American stereotype) than did participants in the control condition ($M = 7.08, SD = 1.42$), $t(66) = 2.56, p < .05$. Furthermore, participants in the directed and spontaneous suppression conditions did not signifi-

cantly differ from each other, $t(66) = .75$, $p = .72$. (Wyer, Sherman, & Stroessner, 1998, p. 347)

The following contrast analysis provides more information about how the contrasts were set up than does the previous example. This can be very helpful to interested readers who would like to do something similar in their own research. Notice that r was reported as an effect size indicator.

> A contrast analysis (Rosenthal and Rosnow, 1985) was performed to test the specific guilt by message type interaction that was predicted. A contrast of +2 was assigned to the guilt, positive self-feeling message condition; – 2 was assigned to the no guilt, positive self-feeling condition, +1 was assigned to the guilt, direct request message, and –1 was assigned to the not guilt, direct request message condition. This analysis indicated that there was a substantial effect for the predicted interaction model ($F(1, 56) = 4.25$, $p < .05$, $r = .26$), and that there was a trivial amount of residual explained variation ($F(2, 56) < 1.00$, ns). Thus, this analysis indicated that the data are consistent with predictions. (Boster et al., 1999, pp. 173–174)

Trend Analysis

Trend analysis tests for a particular trend in the data (linear, quadratic, cubic). You will need to identify the shape of the trend you are testing and report the observed test value, significance level, and effect size. The following is a good example that includes a report of effect size.

> More important, the ANOVA revealed a large main effect for strategy level, $F(8, 1120) = 118.89$, $p < .001$, $\eta^2 = .46$. To examine the main effect of strategy level on masculinity ratings further, a trend analysis was conducted. The linear trend was significant, $F(1, 140) = 191.45$, $p < .001$, and accounted for 32.51% of the within-subjects variation (and 70.79% of the between-strategy level variation) for masculinity ratings. (Kunkel & Burleson, 1999, p. 319)

Log Transformation and Trend Analysis

Although log transformations can be used with many types of statistical procedures, we have included the following example of an ANOVA with trend analysis because it provides a clear justification and description of transforming the data. Note that the authors make it very clear that the analysis was conducted on "the log of the total number." This simple statement eliminates confusion and could save you a round of revisions. Although we don't reproduce the table and figure mentioned in this next example, the report provides a model of how you can make text and other elements work together. This example also does a nice job of "translating" the findings with a single sentence at the end of the paragraph. Also, remember to include effect size when you report your analysis.

The number of hurricane-relevant propositions generated by children as a function of age and storm severity is shown in Table 2. They ranged from 21 to 554, with an overall (unweighted) mean of 153.6 (SD = 93.8). In general, children spoke a great deal about the hurricane related events. Because the distribution was skewed, log transforms were performed and the log (base 10) of the total number of propositions generated served as our primary dependent measure (see Table 2).

Is there a relation between stress and amount recalled and is it affected by age? An ANOVA was conducted with child age (3 or 4 years) and storm severity (high, moderate, and low) on the log of the total number of hurricane-relevant propositions recalled. Results indicated a main effect of child age with 4-year-olds recalling significantly more than 3-year-olds, $F(1,94) = 10.32, p = .002$ (see means in Table 2). This difference occurs even though developmental differences in the language production of 3- and 4-year-olds were partly minimized by excluding elaborations from this measure (such as the "big, bad" storm) and by evaluating elaborations separately (see below). Of even greater interest, a significant main effect of hurricane severity was found, $F(2, 94) = 3.14$, $p = .048$. Trend analyses were performed to assess the nature of the relationship between stress and memory. Results indicated a significant quadratic trend, $F(1,94) = 5.84$, $p = .018$, relating the amount recalled and stress (as shown in Figure 1) and no linear trend, $F(1, 94) = 1.46, p > .1$. The moderate severity group recalled the most about the hurricane, whereas those in the low and high severity recalled the least. (Bahrick, Parker, Fishuv, & Levitt, 1998, p. 317)

ANCOVA

What to Report (in addition to ANOVA)
- Adjusted means (adj M)
- Covariate information (regression format)

Suggested Syntax
- *For main effects and interactions:*
  F (df$_B$, df$_W$) = observed F value, significance level, ES (accompanied by a table of adjusted group and cell means and standard deviations).
- *For covariate analyses:* F (df$_B$, df$_W$) = observed F value, significance level, partial ES (after covariates are removed). Accompanying table of pooled within-cell intercorrelations among the covariates and the dependent variable.

Note: Analysis of covariance (ANOVA) allows for the comparison of group means on a dependent variable after the group means have been adjusted on a relevant covariate variable. Reporting ANCOVA results is similar to reporting ANOVA results, except that adjusted means and F ratio derived from those means need to be stated. Notice that as analyses or the research designs increase in complexity, reports of analyses necessarily increase dramatically in length.

Examples from the Literature

The following study, which examines campaign coverage in a mayoral campaign, contains all of the elements necessary when reporting results of an ANCOVA. It is not clear in this example if the reported means are adjusted or observed. You need to indicate clearly that you are reporting adjusted means (e.g., "adjusted M = 4.23"). Also, notice how the covariate is reported in a regression format with the standardized regression coefficient (β) and corresponding *t* test. Remember that tables are also helpful when attempting to report complex or detailed information. Notice that the covariate is clearly indicated toward the top of Table 7.1. See Chapter 8 for more information on constructing tables.

> H1 predicted that those who received the strategy-framed campaign coverage would use more strategy-oriented clauses in describing the Philadelphia mayoral campaign than those who received the issue-framed campaign coverage. Table [7.1] presents the results of two ANCOVA tests. The first column of Table [7.1] indicates that, after adjustment by the covariate, the main effect of newspaper viewing remained significant ($F[1, 135] = 6.57, p < .01$). Those who read strategy-framed print news about the mayoral campaign ($M = 1.01, n = 70$) were more likely to employ strategy-oriented clauses in illustrating the campaign than those who read issue-framed print materials ($M = 0.67, n = 73$). The strength of the association between newspaper viewing and the dependent measure was not strong with a partial $\eta^2 = .05$. The reason for this is that the covariate accounted for most of the variance in the dependent measure. Indeed, the number of words in the posttest significantly covaried with strategy interpretations ($\beta = .46, t[134] = 6.16, p < .001$). This covariate alone explained 22% of the variance in strategy interpretation.
>
> In addition, the main effect of strategy knowledge was found to be significant ($F[1, 135] = 5.51, p < .05$, partial $\eta^2 = .04$). Individuals with high strategy knowledge ($M = 1.07, n = 76$) were more likely to be influenced by exposure to the news materials than those with low strategic campaign knowledge ($M = 0.58, n = 70$). The main effect of broadcast viewing and other interaction effects did not approach significance.
>
> The second column of Table [7.1] shows the framing effects of the issue-framed campaign coverage. The pattern of the findings was the same as in the previous analysis. The main effect of print frame was significant ($F[1, 135] = 3.98, p < .05$, partial $\eta^2 = .03$), that is, those who received issue-framed print materials ($M = 1.66, n = 73$) were more likely to use issue-oriented clauses in describing the campaign than those who received strategy-framed news ($M = 1.23, n = 70$). Again, the main effects of broadcast viewing and the interaction effects were not significant. However, the covariate (word count in the letters) was significantly correlated with the dependent measure ($\beta = .48, t[135] = 6.38, p < .001$). In addition, this researcher

noted a borderline effect of issue knowledge on issue interpretations ($F[1, 135] = 3.51$, $p = .06$, partial $\eta^2 = .03$). Those who had developed issue-oriented campaign knowledge ($M = 1.82$, $n = 73$) were more likely to be influenced by exposure to news materials than individuals with low issue knowledge ($M = 1.06$, $n = 70$).

Overall, the hypothesized framing effects were found for the print news materials. After adjusting for the strong effect of the covariate, the main effect of the print news material remained significant. However, the study revealed no comparable effects for the broadcast news materials. The interaction hypotheses were not supported. Instead, the research showed the main effect of knowledge on interpretation. That is, individuals with high strategic campaign knowledge used more strategic ideas in their narratives,

TABLE 7.1   ANCOVA of Strategy and Issue Interpretations in the Broadcast–Print Experiment

Source	df	Strategy Interpretation F	Issue Interpretation F
Covariate			
Total word counts	1	37.92***	40.69***
Main effects			
Print frame	1	6.57**	3.98*
Broadcast frame	1	1.07	.55
Knowledge differentiation	1	5.51**	3.51
Interactions			
Print X broadcast	1	.12	.24
Print X knowledge	1	.09	.04
Broadcast X knowledge	1	.09	.47
Error	134	(0.83)	(1.43)

Note. Values enclosed in parentheses represent mean square errors. From "Strategy and Issue Frames in Election Campaign Coverage: A Social Cognitive Account of Framing Effects," by J. W. Rhee, 1997, *Journal of Communication, 47* (3), pp. 39–41. Used by permission of Oxford University Press.

*p < .05. **p < .01. ***p < .001.

and individuals with high issue-oriented campaign knowledge used more issue-related ideas in their narratives. (Rhee, 1997, pp. 39–41)

Multivariate Analysis of Variance (MANOVA)

What to Report
- Multivariate statistic (Wilks lambda, Pillais (varies))
- Degrees of freedom (between and within) (df_B / df_W)
- Observed F value (F)
- Significance level (p)
- Effect size (ES, varies with test)
- Univariate effects (see ANOVA)

Supporting information
(reported in text or table)
- Number of observations (N)
- Number of observations per cell (n)
- Descriptive statistics (M and SD)

Suggested Syntax
- Wilks lambda = observed λ value, $F(df_B, df_W)$ = observed F value, significance level, ES

Suggested Format
- The 2 × 3 between groups MANOVA revealed that the multivariate main effect was supported, Wilks lambda = .24, $F(2, 63) = 12.47$, $p < .01$, $\eta^2 = .17$.

Example from the Literature

This example is well organized and includes the important elements necessary for a complete results section. Of the multivariate statistics used to test main effects and interaction in MANOVA, Wilks lambda is the most commonly reported. Although effect size was reported for the multivariate main effect, it was not reported for either of the univariate effect tests. It is recommended that you state effect size for these tests as well. Descriptive statistics were reported elsewhere in the article.

> The multivariate main effect for status, Wilks lambda = .86, $F(12, 542) = 3.52$, $p < .001$, $R^2 = .14$, was accompanied by significant univariate effects on blocking and avoidance, $F(2, 276) = 8.85$, $p < .001$, and confrontation $F(2, 276) = 7.39$, $p < .001$. Subordinates reported using significantly more blocking and avoidance and confrontation [strategies] than did either supervisors or co-workers in response to a physical invasion. (LePoire, Burgoon, & Parrott, 1992, pp. 427–428)

MANOVA with Bartlett's Test of Sphericity

This example reports a Bartlett's test, a test of the assumption of the sphericity of the data, which tends to be very sensitive in detecting correlations among the dependent variables. An alternative is to view the correlation matrix between dependent variables. Notice how Wilks lambda is reported after the multivariate main effect syntax.

> Analysis of observer perceptions of target's arousal confirmed H1; perceived arousal changed after the manipulation was enacted. The multivariate main effect for immediacy manipulation onset on all three types of arousal—general, negative, and positive—was significant, $F(6, 40) = 2.99$, $p < .05$, Wilks's $\lambda = .69$ (Bartlett's test of sphericity = 45.41, $p < .001$, average $r = .42$), as were univariate curvilinear contrasts: general arousal, $F(1, 45) = 8.82$, $p < .01$, $\eta^2 = .16$; negative arousal, $F(1, 45) = 7.84$, $p < .01$, $\eta^2 = .15$; and positive arousal, $F(1, 45) = 10.43$, $p = .001$, $\eta^2 = .19$. All forms of arousal were perceived as highest immediately following the onset of the immediacy manipulation (see Figure 1) [not shown here], as expected in H1. (Andersen, Guerrero, Buller, & Jorgensen, 1998, p. 519)

MANCOVA

What to Report (in addition to MANOVA)
- Adjusted means (adj M)
- Covariate information (regression format)

Note: Multivariate analysis of covariance (MANCOVA) allows for the comparison of group means on more than one dependent variable after the group means have been adjusted on one or more relevant covariate variable. Reporting MANCOVA results is similar to reporting MANOVA results, except that adjusted means and *F* ratio derived from those means need to be stated. Refer to the suggested syntax for MANOVA and ANCOVA to report your MANCOVA.

Example from the Literature

The results of this MANCOVA contains Pillais, univariate, and simple effects tests. The simple effects tests were reported to show where the point of significance was in the interaction. Adjusted means were not identified in this example. Be sure to identify clearly that you are using adjusted means. The effect of the covariate is also not reported in this example. See ANCOVA for an example of how to report your covariate in both the text and table format.

> Scores obtained from the Just World Scale were categorized into quartiles in order to compare participants with the highest and lowest levels of JWS. A MANCOVA was run controlling for the age of the participants with the level of JWS (highest or lowest quartile), the sex of the participant, the sex of the victim, and the sexual orientation of the victim as the independent variables, and the variables relating to the victim's responsibility and fault as the dependent variables. There was a main effect for the sex of the victim $(F(2, 31) = 5.17, p < .012)$. A Univariate F test found a significant effect on perceptions of the victim's fault with respondents perceiving the victim as being more at fault $(M = 1.70)$ if the victim were a woman, than if the victim were a man $(M = 1.60)$, $F(1, 32) = 9.49$, $p = .004$. A Pillais test of the model found a significant two-way interaction effect for the sex of the participant and the sex of the victim $(F(2, 31) = 4.85, p < .015)$. Univariate F tests on each of the dependent variables found a significant effect on perceptions of the victim's fault $(F(1, 31) = 8.34, p < .007)$ but no significant effect on victim's responsibility. Simple effects tests showed that men perceived the female victim $(M = 1.88)$ as significantly more at fault than the male victim $(M = 1.56)$. (Ford, Liwag-McLamb, & Foley, 1998, pp. 258–259)

Regression and Multiple Regression

What to Report   *Overall Model*
- Multiple R (R)
- Effect size (R^2)
- Adjusted R^2 (adj R^2)
- Observed F (F)
- Degrees of freedom (df)
- Significance level (p)

Predictors
- Unstandardized regression coefficient (B)
- Standardized regression coefficient (β)
- Observed t value (t)
- Significance level (p)
- Semipartial correlations (variance accounted for per variable)

Suggested Syntax
- *For the model:* $F(\text{df}_B, \text{df}_W)$ = observed F value, significance level, R^2, adj R^2 (accompanied by table with unstandardized regression coefficient, standardized regression coefficients).
- *Individual relationships between the independent variables and dependent variables:* t = observed t value, significance level, effect size.

Suggested Format
- A standard multiple regression analysis was performed between the dependent variable (purchase intention) and the independent variables (story value, cover design, attitude toward the magazine). Analysis was performed using SPSS REGRESSION.
   Assumptions were tested by examining normal probability plots of

residuals and scatter diagrams of residuals versus predicted residuals. No violations of normality, linearity, or homoscedasticity of residuals were detected. In addition, box plots revealed no evidence of outliers.

Regression analysis revealed that the model significantly predicted magazine purchase intention, $F(6, 562) = 27.78, p < .001$. R^2 for the model was .46, and adjusted R^2 was .44. Table 1 displays the unstandardized regression coefficients (B), intercept, and standardized regression coefficients (β) for each variable.

In terms of individual relationships between the independent variables and purchase intention, story value ($t = 7.90$, $p < .001$), cover design ($t = 5.17, p < .001$), and attitude toward the magazine ($t = 6.63, p < .001$) each significantly predicted purchase intention (see Table 1 for means and standard deviations). Together, those three variables contributed 41.3% in shared variability. Most germane to this current study, however, story value contributed 4.5% in shared variability with the dependent variable.

Note: Because of the more complex nature of multiple regression, we have expanded the suggested format section. Multiple regression is an extension of simple linear regression and more common. If you need to report a simple regression, use the suggested format as a general guideline. Regarding multiple regression, you will need to clearly identify the type of regression analysis employed (e.g., "a standard multiple regression model was performed"). Report results of the overall model followed by additional analyses. A table is an effective way to summarize the findings of your regression analysis.

Example from the Literature

The following brief example provides the basics of what is reported in a regression results section. Postmes, Branscombe, Spears, and Young (1999) also incorporate a summary of their findings in this example.

> This suggestion was confirmed in a regression analysis with the personal–group discrepancy as the dependent measure and the two direct comparison measures as predictors. The two predictors explain a sizable proportion of variance, $R^2 = .20$, $F(2, 192) = 24.98$, $p < .01$. The intergroup comparison's relation with the discrepancy ($\beta = -.34$, $p < .01$) is of similar magnitude to the interpersonal comparison's ($\beta = .32$, $p < .01$). It appears that both comparisons explain a part of the discrepancy, which is consistent with our hypothesis that the personal–group discrepancy is composed of two distinct comparative judgments. (Postmes, Branscombe, Spears, & Young, 1999, p. 327)

In the original text, R^2 appeared as r^2, possibly as a result of a typographic error or an error in the copyediting process.

Stepwise Multiple Regression

This example of a stepwise multiple regression reports both significant and nonsignificant findings. Notice that the author is very clear in explaining what variables are tested and the resulting statistical findings. In this excerpt, R^2 and adjusted R^2 are not reported. You should include both in your report.

> Based on sociological notions that baby boomers are vulnerable to collective nostalgic products from the 1950s and 1960s, the present study was an empirical test of that concept. The results of this investigation illustrate that reruns from the 1950s and 1960s do not provide the best model for predicting rerun viewing among the baby boomers. Also, no significant relationship was found between baby boomers and any decade of rerun programs. Therefore, the hypothesis that baby boomers would have preferences for viewing reruns from more recent eras was not supported. However, results of the stepwise multiple regression show the 16–25 age cohort was significantly related to reruns of the 1980s,

$F(1, 487) = 14.27$, $R = .17$, beta $= .31$, $p < .05$, and the 1970s, $F(1, 487) = 21.25$, $R = .29$, beta $= .35$, $p < .05$. The 55–65 age cohort was significantly related to reruns of the 1980s, $F(1, 487) = 9.48$, $R = .20$, beta $= .23$, $p < .05$, and the 26–35 age cohort was significantly related to reruns of the 1980s, $F(1, 487) = 20.07$, $R = .21$, beta $= .29$, $p < .05$. Baby boomers (36–45) did not enter the stepwise multiple regression for any of the four decades of programming, and the 1950s and 1960s decade did not show any age cohort entries. (Furno-Lamude, 1994, pp. 133–134)

Hierarchical Multiple Regression

The following example by Pfau et al. (1997) reports the results of a hierarchical multiple regression that tests the influence of communication modalities on candidate perceptions during a primary. This is a good example of describing the blocks entered into the design. Note that tables are not included with this example and that variance accounted for is reported not as R^2, but in text form.

> We employed hierarchical multiple regression to test the relative influence of communication modalities on respondents' perceptions of the candidates. Respondent demographics, a control variable that consisted of gender, education, and strength of political party affiliation, were entered in the first block. Use of communication modalities was entered in the second block. Interactions involving communication modality and the number of days from the New Hampshire primary to the prospective voters' own primary election was entered in the third block. Regression results are summarized for each candidate and examined in detail in the context of the specific hypotheses.
>
> For candidate Bob Dole, the full regression equation with control variables, communication modalities, and interaction terms was significant on all four dependent variables: attitude, $F(13,222) = 3.54$, $p < .001$; competence, $F(13,232) = 4.05$, $p < .001$; relationals, $F(13,195) = 4.08$, $p < .001$; and emotion, $F(13,216) = 2.58$, $p < .01$. The full model was responsible for considerable variance in these variables: 17%, 18%, 21%, and 13%, respectively.
>
> The results identified one control variable, strength of party affiliation, as a predictor of voters' perceptions of Bob Dole. Betas were positive for all four dependent variables, and suggest that more partisan Republican identifiers manifested more positive

perceptions of Dole. The results, including those for communication modalities (analyzed below) are displayed in Table 1. (Pfau et al., 1997, pp. 14–15)

Tables often work hand-in-hand with the text of a results section. Here is a good example of how this can be done. These authors do a good job describing the procedure of two hierarchical multiple regression analyses.

> To test the relationship between perceived social support, perceived quality of parental relationships and acceptance, two hierarchical regressions were performed using the PBI Care scores for mother and father as dependent variables. These regressions were performed to assess whether the PAS Mother and Father acceptance scores predict unique variance following the removal of the effects of two global support measures (SSQS and PSS-Family) and the SSQ relationship-specific support scores for mother and father. Each regression took the same form, with sex entered on the first step, the social support scores entered second and the PAS Mother and Father scores entered on the last step.
>
> The results of these regressions are presented in Table [7.2]. Sex was not a significant predictor of Mother Care or Father Care (both $ps > .10$). When the social support scores were added in the second step, they predicted an additional 59 percent ($p < .001$) of variance in the Mother Care score and an additional 53 percent ($p < .001$) of the variance in the Father Care score. Following these gains, the PAS Mother and Father acceptance scores accounted for 16 and 20 percent unique variance (both $ps < .001$) in the Mother Care and Father Care scores, respectively. Inspection of the squared semi-partial correlations in the prediction of Mother Care revealed that only the PAS Mother acceptance score predicted significant unique variance ($r_{sp}^2 = .11, p < .001$). Similarly, only the PAS Father score predicted unique variance in Father Care ($r_{sp}^2 = .16$, $p < .001$). (Brock, Sarason, Sanghvi, & Gurung, 1998, pp. 14–16)

Logistic Regression

What to Report   *Overall Model*
- Observed χ^2 value (χ^2)
- Effect size (R^2)

TABLE 7.2   Hierarchical Regressions of Perceived Global Social Support, Sex, and Acceptance on the Parental Bonding Instrument's Mother Care and Father Care Scores

	Dependent Measures							
	PBI Mother Care				PBI Father Care			
	R^2 Chng.	F-Value	β	sp^2	R^2 Chng.	F-Value	β	sp^2
Step 1								
Sex	.00	<1.0	.09	.01	.01	<1.0	.16	.02**
Step 2								
Perceived social support								
SSQS			−.01	.00			−.05	.00
SSQ Mother			.23	.02**			−.12	.00
SSQ Father			−.16	.01*			.17	.01*
PSS-Family			.23	.03**			.31	.05***
R^2 Chng.	.59***	38.76			.53***	29.59		
Step 3								
Acceptance scores								
Mother			.57	.11***			−.03	.00
Father			.05	.00			.62	.16***
R^2 Chng.	.16***	34.05			.20***	37.04		
R^2 Tot. (adj)	.75***				>74***			

Two-tailed tests of significance: *** $p < .001$; ** $p < .01$; * $p < .05$

Note. From "The Perceived Acceptance Scale: Development and Validation," by D. M. Brock, I. G. Sarason, H. Sanghvi, & R. A. R. Gurung, 1998, *Journal of Social and Personal Relationships, 15,* pp. 14–16. Reprinted by permission of Sage Publications.

- Degrees of freedom (df)
- Number of observations (*N*)
- Significance level (*p*)
- Classification results (optional)

Predictors
- Standardized regression coefficient (β)
- Observed Wald χ^2 value (χ^2)
- Significance level (*p*)
- Odds ratio

Suggested Syntax ■ R^2 = observed R^2 value, χ^2 (df, *N* = number of observations) = observed χ^2 value, significance level

Suggested Format ■ R^2 = .23, χ^2 (1, *N* = 178) = 12.71, $p < .01$

Note: Refer to the section on regression for general guidelines for reporting logistic regression. Note, however, that the suggested syntax for logistic regression is similar to that of the chi-square test.

Example from the Literature

Below is an example of a logistic regression that uses a table to support the report of the results. Note in the second paragraph that researchers report the alpha level. This set of results also provides the reader with odds ratios and Wald test values. What is missing is the R^2 value for the overall model, which needs to be reported to make the description of your regression complete.

> Logistic regression analysis was employed to predict the probability that a participant would approve the continuation of the research. The predictor variables were participant's gender, idealism, relativism, and four dummy variables coding the scenario. The continuous predictor variables were approximately normally distributed within each of the dependent groups, and the variances were stable. Logistic regression was chosen over discriminant function analysis because we wanted to evaluate simultaneously the effects of two continuous predictors, one dichotomous predictor, and one

qualitative predictor. A test of the full model versus a model with intercept only was statistically significant, χ^2 (7, $N = 315$) = 87.51, $p < .001$. The model was able correctly to classify 73% of those who approved continuing the research and 70% of those who did not, for an overall success rate of 71%.

Table [7.3] shows the logistic regression coefficient, Wald test, and odds ratio for each of the predictors. Employing a .05 criterion of statistical significance, gender, idealism, relativism, and two of the scenario dummy variables had significant partial effects. The odds ratio for gender indicates that when holding other variables constant, a man is 3.5 times more likely to approve the research than is a woman. (Wuensch & Poteat, 1988, p. 145)

TABLE 7.3   Logistic Regression Predicting Decision from Gender, Ideology, and Scenario

Predictor	β	Wald χ^2	p	Odds Ratio
Gender	1.25	20.59	< .001	3.51
Idealism	−.70	37.89	< .001	.50
Relativism	.33	6.63	.01	1.39
Scenario				
Cosmetic	−.71	2.85	.091	.49
Theory	−1.16	7.35	.007	.31
Meat	−.87	4.16	.041	.42
Veterinary	−.54	1.75	.186	.58

Note. From "Evaluating the Morality of Animal Research: Effects of Ethical Ideology, Gender, and Purpose," by K. L. Wuensch & G. M. Poteat, 1998, *Journal of Social Behavior and Personality, 13*, p. 145.

CHAPTER

8 Presenting Results Visually

Using Tables

Tables are ubiquitous in social science journals focusing on the presentation of the results of empirical, quantitative studies—and for good reason. Tables can make data easier to understand because, if done correctly, the data are not only well organized, but they also invite comparisons and observations that may interest the reader beyond the hypotheses investigated by the study.

The purpose of tables, according to Wainer (1997), is four-fold: First, tables serve an exploratory function. Data can contain answers to questions that may be explicit in the viewer's mind. In other words, tables can serve a heuristic function in that they can generate greater interest in the data and other questions that might be answered by this or future studies.

Second, tables have a communication function: Once data are explored, they can be displayed to convey what has been discovered to a broader audience. Tables condense data into a form that can make them easier to understand.

Third, tables serve a storage function. Because data are expensive to gather, it makes sense that summary forms of the data exist as a precaution against loss. Tables also often allow the replication of statistical analyses by other interested readers. In this way, tables allow the transference of the data in aggregate form.

Finally, tables also have a decorative function. They are often used to enliven a presentation. Tables attract the eye of the reader and break up the text of an article. In this way, tables invite greater participation by the reader.

What Should Be Contained in a Table?

There are some (nearly) universal elements that should appear in your table. It is important to mention that the exact contents of your table will vary by the statistical analyses you are performing and/or the hypotheses you are testing. Some statistical analyses, (such as multiple regression) almost never appear without accompanying tables, whereas other reports of analyses include all relevant information in the text of the results section. Rudestam and Newton (1992) offer some guidelines for what should appear in a table.

1. Table number. Generally speaking, your tables should be numbered as whole numbers (Table 1, Table 2, etc.), not in a chapter number–table number format (like 3.1, 3.2, etc.). However, tables done for dissertations or book chapters may have to correspond to the requirements of the publisher or graduate college.

2. The table name or title that includes the name of the variable of interest (one or more of your dependent variables) and some information about the independent variable and/or the population involved in the study. Example: The effect of cigarette smoking on the academic performance of teenagers. Generally speaking, your table will correspond to the essence of your investigation as a whole or to specific hypotheses.

3. The set of mutually exclusive and exhaustive categories. By completing step 2 or by writing up your results section, you will have gained a clearer picture of what these categories will be. These categories usually appear in the rows of your table.

4. Table headings. It is common for the columns of your table to correspond to common statistics, such as means, standard deviations, percentages, F values, degrees of freedom, and/or significance levels.

5. The information in the body of the table corresponding to the information you acquired during the process of data analysis.

6. Notes, including the source, if the data are not original.

Table Notation

Sometimes it is necessary or desirable to use notation instead of text or even numbers. There are three types of notes, including general notes, specific notes, and probability notes. General notes appear at the bottom of a table and include information about the table as a whole, as well as the meaning of symbols or abbreviations. Specific notes refer to the content of only one specific cell and are assigned superscript lowercase letters, beginning with the letter *a*. The order of assignment begins in the upper left of a table and proceeds across rows.

Probability notes are used in place of a separate column for the significance level of the test statistic (the *p* value) and use an asterisk *. One asterisk corresponds to the lowest level of significance set for the study (usually .05, but sometimes .10), whereas two asterisks indicate a higher level of significance, and so on. Thus, it is common for a table to have probability notes that look like

$* p < .05$
$** p < .01$
$*** p < .001$

Sometimes, the use of an asterisk also indicates whether a test is one-tailed or two-tailed. For example, it is not unusual for the value of a test statistic to have an asterisk, with the corresponding note reading

$* p < .05$, one-tailed

If you create more than one table to present your results, but your notation remains the same, you must still renote each table. In other words, it is not enough to note that one asterisk indicates significance at a .05 level on the first table and assume that your reader will remember that notation for all subsequent tables. It may seem redundant to say the same thing at the bottom of each table, but it is necessary in this case.

Some Principles for Developing Tables

There are some commonsense and some not so commonsense principles that can help you organize a table. First, don't try to do too much. Through clever design, it's possible to present the results of various hypotheses in a single table. However, unless the hypotheses are closely related, this may not be advisable. On the other hand, related analyses should appear in the same table if at all possible. Modeling your tables after published exemplars of similar research may be the best help in striking this balance until you develop a breadth of experience.

Second, use white space effectively. White space is a relief to the eye and actually aids comprehension by reducing potential confusion. The best tables present information efficiently and with clarity. Tables can range in size from a few lines of data to two or more pages; the measure of a good table is not how much information is presented but how clearly a picture of the data is presented.

Third, tables and text should refer to each other. However, not everything contained in a table needs to appear in the text. Follow the guidelines that appear in the chapter corresponding to the statistical results you are presenting for information about what needs to appear in the text of your results section. Tables can, and often do, present a greater amount of information.

Finally, if you are submitting your work to a journal that uses APA guidelines, every line in your table must be double-spaced. However, other purposes may not require you to double-space.

Here are some other guidelines that will help you construct a table:

1. Order and group rows and columns by some aspect of the data, such as size (largest to smallest or vice versa), chronology (first observation to the last), or according to interest (placing some set of rows or columns next to each other to invite easy comparison).

2. If appropriate, frame the display with summary statistics. Summaries of rows and columns are important as a standard of comparison. Common summary statistics include sums, means, and/or medians. These are easier to understand when they are visually different from the individual entries and set apart spatially.

3. Values are compared down columns more easily than across rows.

4. Round numbers heavily. Research shows that comprehension rises as the number of digits presented is reduced. The convention for published social science research is to round to two decimal places.

5. When creating a table to be part of a manuscript that will be submitted for publication, be sure that the entire table is double-spaced (unless otherwise specified by the journal or editor).

Constructing Tables

We strongly suggest using the TABLES command in your word processor to create tables. Learning this procedure will take a small investment of your time, but will pay off almost immediately: You will soon discover that it is much easier to keep your columns properly aligned, especially if you make any changes whatsoever to your document. Even a small change such as changing font size or type, line spacing, or margins will throw off a tabbed table. However, a table created with a TABLES command will not suffer these difficulties. Moreover, you will find that you can make much more attractive tables with the appropriate borders with this command.

In this section, we will present some examples of the most commonly used tables, including frequency, bivariate, and contingency tables; ANOVA tables; correlation matrices; reliability tables; and regression tables. Additional examples of tables also appear in chapters on some individual statistics.

Frequency and Bivariate Tables.

These are probably the simplest tables to create. The most common frequency tables contain the categories of interest in the first column, followed by the frequency and (often) the percentage of the sample this number represents. Frequency tables commonly present means and information about standard deviations as well.

A bivariate table is also called a cross-tabulation or contingency table. It is usually presented in form of a square or rectangle with rows representing one variable and columns representing categories of another variable. Each variable may have more than two levels. For example, you might want to present information on income as a function of education; each variable may have four or five (or more) levels, but this would still be considered a bivariate table. The form of the table often looks like this:

Levels of Y	Levels of X (IV)		Row Totals
	x1	x2	
y1			
y2			
y3			
Column Totals			Grand Total

The values in each cell represent the number of times (frequency) that that pair of values occurred. The marginal frequencies are the total number for that single row or column. Table 8.1 reports the frequency of the levels of only one variable (frequency of church attendance), but also reports the percentages of each level.

TABLE 8.1   Frequency of Attendance at Religious Services

	f	%
Never	254	17.2
Less than once a year	108	7.3
Once a year	168	11.3
Several times a year	194	13.1
Once a month	116	7.8
2–3 times a month	143	9.7
Nearly every week	109	7.4
Every week	277	18.7
More than once a week	109	7.4
Don't know/no answer	3	0.2
Total	1,481	100.0

Note. From National Opinion Research Center General Social Survey, 1988. In *Surviving Your Dissertation: A Comprehensive Guide to Content and Process* (p. 103), by K. E. Rudestam & R. R. Newton, 1992, Newbury Park: Sage. Copyright 1992 by Sage Publications, Inc.

This next bivariate table (Table 8.2) describes components of the American dream myth featured in the news stories of the prominent black paper, the *Chicago Defender,* at a particular point in the migration of blacks to the North. This table is organized so that the categories of dream themes are listed from greatest to least frequency. Note that this table presents frequencies without any other accompanying information. This may be all that your reporting requirements entail.

TABLE 8.2 Frequency of American Dream Themes in the Discontent Stage

Dream Themes	1915	1916	1917	1918	1919	Total
1) Freedom (moral)	32	19	13	23	22	109
2) Equality (moral)	8	12	3	7	5	35
3) Democracy (moral)	1	3	4	4	4	16
4) Wealth (material)	0	3	4	3	4	14
5) Work ethic (material)	1	0	0	5	3	9
6) New beginnings (material)	1	0	2	2	1	6
7) Religious independence (moral)	0	0	0	0	2	2
8) Consumption (material)	0	0	0	0	0	0
Total	43	37	26	44	41	191

Note. From "Selling the American Dream Myth to Black Southerners: The *Chicago Defender* and the Great Migration of 1915–1919" by A. DeSantis, 1998, *Western Journal of Communication, 62,* p. 484.

Chi-square analyses are often accompanied by contingency tables (also called cross-tabulation). Contingency tables report the frequencies of variables according to two sets of values of categorical variables. Table 8.3 reports percentages rather than frequencies and provides column totals.

TABLE 8.3   Human Rights Coverage by Story Byline

	Staff	Stringer	News Service (with id.)	Not Identified
Human rights	34%	45%	21%	29%
Other stories	66%	55%	79%	71%
Total	267	51	203	120
N = 641				
Chi-square = 12.7	*p* < .001	d.f. = 2		
Cramer's *V* = .14	*p* < .001			

Note. From "U.S. Newspaper Coverage of Human Rights in Latin America, 1975–1982: Exploring President Carter's Agenda-Building Influence" by C. Cassara, 1998, *Journalism and Mass Communication Quarterly, 75*, p. 483.

This next example, Table 8.4, reverses where the totals appear on the variable of interest. First, the author reports the frequency in each cell, then translates the row total into a percentage.

TABLE 8.4   Candidate Attacks by Time Period

Time Period	Candidate Did Not Attack	Candidate Attacked	PercentageTime a Candidate Attacked
Pre-primary	285	24	8%
Initial contests	119	73	38%
Three-way competition	14	15	52%
Two-way competition before New York primary	11	25	70%
Two-way competition after New York primary*	94	4	4%

Note. Does not include attacks on the incumbent president of the opposition party (George Bush). Cell entries for attacks in the Pre-primary and Post–New York periods would increase by 8 and 12, respectively. During the competitive portion of the nomination campaign approximately 49 percent of the cases involved an attack of one candidate on an intra-party opponent. Inclusion of the non-competitive portions lowers the percentage to 26 percent. From "Attack Politics in Presidential Nomination Campaigns: An Examination of the Frequency and Determinants of Intermediated Negative Messages against Opponents," by A. A. Haynes & S. L. Rhine, 1998, *Political Research Quarterly, 51*, p. 704. Reprinted by permission of the University of Utah.

This last contingency table (Table 8.5) reports the *n* size, means, and standard deviations, but no other statistical information (which the authors have elected to present in the text).

TABLE 8.5   Mean Number of Novel Propositions and Novelty Judgments by Age Group and Medium

Creative-Imagination Measures	Grades 1–2 (n = 32)		Grades 3–4 (n = 32)	
	Radio	TV	Radio	TV
Number of novel propositions				
M	12.56	13.22	25.94	22.38
SD	9.26	7.56	15.85	13.89
Novelty judgments				
M	34.59	36.72	49.63	45.59
SD	13.01	13.34	13.61	13.59

Note. From "Children's Creative Imagination in Responses to Radio and Television Stories," by P. M. Valkenburg & J. W. J. Beentjes, 1997, *Journal of Communication, 47*, p. 22. Used by permission of Oxford University Press.

ANOVA/MANOVA Tables

ANOVA tables often appear in the social science literature. Whereas the text of a results section includes most of the important information, an ANOVA table provides some additional information that may be of interest to your readers, including the Sum of Squares (SS) and the Means Squared (MS). Although there are significant variations in how much of this information appears in a publication, the form of an ANOVA table usually looks like this:

Table Title

Source	SS	df	MS	F	p
Variable 1					
Variable 2					
Var. 1 × Var. 2					
Residual					
Total					

Here's an excellent example of several one-way ANOVAs presented as a table (Table 8.6). However, note that an effect size is not reported in this example. This could be fixed easily by simply adding one more column for eta-squared. Additionally, nonsignificant results do not need a separate column, but can be reported under *p*.

TABLE 8.6   One-Way Analysis of Variance for Crisis Type by Attribution Dimension

| | Crisis Type | | | | | | | |
| | Accident | | Transgression | | | | | |
Variable	M	SD	M	SD	F	df	p	ns
Locus	6.01	1.54	7.45	1.42	66.66	1,275	<.001	
External control	5.09	1.73	5.28	1.64	.85	1,275		.35
Stability	4.25	1.26	4.16	1.55	.27	1,275		.60

Note. From "Communication and Attributions in a Crisis: An Experimental Study in Crisis Communication," by W. T. Coombs & S. J. Holladay, 1996, *Journal of Public Relations Research, 8,* p. 291.

Here's an excerpt of a lengthy table reporting a series of factorial ANOVAs corresponding to the authors' hypotheses (Table 8.7). This will give you some idea of what a classic ANOVA table looks like:

TABLE 8.7   Analysis of Variance Results

Source of Variation	Sum of Squares	d.f.	Mean Square	F	Sig. of F
For Ad					
Main effects	660.64	5	132.13	3.15	.009
Subject gender	202.04	1	202.04	4.82	.029
Type of ad	481.36	4	120.34	2.87	.023
Two-way interactions	454.08	4	113.52	2.71	.030
Explained	1125.83	9	125.09	2.99	.002
Residual	11729.29	280	41.89		
Total	12855.12	289	44.48		

Note. From "Beefcake and Cheesecake: Insights for Advertisers," by M. Y. Jones, A. J. S. Stanaland, & B. D. Gelb, 1998, *Journal of Advertising, 27,* p. 47. © Journal of Advertising.

Contrast analysis is also sometimes presented as a table. Table 8.8 shows an idea of how to organize information on this type of analysis:

TABLE 8.8   Citation Effects in the Exemplification of Poor versus Rich Farmers

| Measure | Farmers[1] | | | | | ANOVA | | Contrast | |
	Poor Cited Rich Para	Poor Cited Rich Cited	Poor Para Rich Para	None Cited None Para	Poor Para Rich Cited	$F_{(4,64)}$	p	$F_{(1,64)}$	p
Blame for misfortune[2]	5.32	5.25	4.47	3.73	3.59	3.39	.014	10.50	.002
Bankruptcy and blame[3]	4.53	4.78	3.80	3.23	3.14	3.30	.016	10.03	.002
Profit and wealth[4]	25.29	22.92	31.67	32.31	34.12	1.75	.151	6.12	.016
Good-Fortune credit[5]	3.88	5.54	4.77	5.08	5.18	1.79	.142	1.49	.227
Informative reporting[6]	4.00	4.22	3.93	3.28	4.16	0.72	.578		
Balanced reporting[7]	5.35	5.79	6.37	6.50	5.88	0.66	.620		

[1]The contrast predictions: PFc-RFp> PFc-RFc>PFp-RFp=Nc-Np>PFp-RFc. Cited = c, Paraphrased = p.

[2]Mean of Banks at Fault and Government at Fault

[3]Mean of Banks at Fault, Government at Fault, and Farm Bankruptcies, with % of the latter divided by 10 ($\alpha = .79$)

[4]Mean of % Profit Farmers and % Wealthy Farmers ($\alpha = .76$)

[5]Mean of Banks Supportive and Government Supportive ($\alpha = .85$)

[6]Mean of Informative, Upsetting, and Entertaining ($\alpha = .90$)

[7]Mean of Balanced and Fair ($\alpha = .64$)

Note. From "Effects of Citation in Exemplifying Testimony on Issue Perception," by R. Gibson & D. Zellman, 1998, *Journalism and Mass Communication Quarterly,* 75, p. 173.

Correlational Analyses and Correlational Matrices

You will have no doubt noticed that a matrix showing the correlations between a set of variables has identical values above and below the "diagonal" of the matrix. In order to make a correlation matrix easier to read, present numbers along only the lower (or upper) half of the diagonal.

The other half of the diagonal need not remain empty, however; standard deviations are sometimes presented in this space. Significance levels can be reported in parentheses below the value of the test statistic (r), or they can be indicated through the use of probability notes. Usually, a single asterisk is used to indicate significance at the .05 level, two asterisks are used to indicate significance at the .01 level, and so on. See the Table Notation section for more information.

The N size (number of cases) may be included elsewhere in the results section, in a table note, or, if there is variation in the n for each pair of variables being correlated, in parentheses below each correlation. Table 8.9 reports only the correlation and the significance.

TABLE 8.9 Pearson Correlations between Prejudice Ratings and Predictor Variables: Stories with Whites in Power

	1	2	3	4	5	6	7	8	9
					P-	P-	V-	V-	Perp-
	Prej	Norm	Turf	Likely	This	Other	This	Other	Pgroup
1. Prej rating		.58*	.07	.61**	.40	.35	−.34	−.25	.57*
2. Norm			−.01	.15	.00	.44	.04	−.44	.50*
3. Turf				−.01	.01	−.00	−.34	−.12	−.31
4. Likely					.49*	.26	−.45	−.05	.47*
5. P-This						.41	−.37	.26	.49*
6. P-Other							−.01	.10	.55*
7. V-This								.48*	−.01
8. V-Other									.03

Note. P-This = Perpetrator's power in this situation; P-Other = Perpetrator's power in other situations; V-This = Victim's power in this situation; V-Other = Victim's power in other situations; Perp-Pgroup = Perpetrator's race matched the group expected to be in power. Higher numbers mean more of that quality. See the text for more detail. From "Perceiving Discrimination: The Role of Prototypes and Norm Violation," by M. L. Inmann, J. Huerta, & S. Oh, 1998, *Social Cognition, 16*, p. 437.

$N = 18$ for each correlation.

* $p < .05$, ** $p < .01$.

Instead of presenting the *N* size in a table note, Table 8.10 provides the *N* in its title. It also provides the means and standard deviations for each scale at the bottom of each column. Note also that the triangle of data is reversed from the previous example.

If you are trying to write up the results of interrater and in-teritem reliabilities, consider Table 8.11 by Burgoon and LePoire (1999). Please note that vocalics is only one of two dimensions that appear in the original table.

TABLE 8.10   Pearson Correlations, Means, and Standard Deviation for Scales (*N* = 79)

Indicant	1	2	3	4	5	6	7	8
Innovativeness	1.00							
Acceptance	.67	1.00						
Communication Quality	.59	.52	1.00					
Slack Resources	.37	.49	.27	1.00				
Prominence	.16	.12	.08	−.13	1.00			
Range	.29	.13	.14	−.04	.77	1.00		
Formalization	.36	.32	.56	.17	−.16	−.09	1.00	
Decentralization	.66	.67	.45	.42	.15	.27	.14	1.00
M	6.33	6.26	6.86	4.36	.01	3.31	7.22	5.45
SD	1.62	1.70	1.47	1.78	.02	5.30	1.38	2.17

Note. From "Testing Two Contrasting Structural Models of Innovativeness in a Contractual Network," by J. D. Johnson, M. E. Meyer, J. M. Berkowitz, C. T. Ethington, & V. D. Miller, 1997, *Human Communication Research, 24,* p. 336. Used by permission of Oxford University Press.

Regression and Multiple Regression Tables

Unfortunately, due to the complexity of multiple regression analyses, no one accepted format has emerged for presenting

TABLE 8.11 Interrater and Interitem Reliabilities
for Nonverbal Ratings

| Dimension and Items | Interrater Reliability | | Interitem Reliability |
	Composites	Items	
VOCALICS			
Global involvement (3 items)	.90		.97
Global pleasantness (3 items)	.87		.96
Expressivity			
Intensity (tempo/pitch)	.71		.77
Pitch variety		.50	
Perceived animation	.87		.99
Conversational management			
Turn length		.91	
Turn pitches		.65	
Fluency		.65	
Relaxation			
Nervous vocalizations		.73	
Relaxed voice (2 items)	.73		.98
Positivity			
Resonance		.91	
Relaxed laughter		.59	

Note. From "Nonverbal Cues and Interpersonal Judgments: Participant and Observer Perceptions of Intimacy, Dominance, Composure and Formality," by J. K. Burgoon & B. A. LePoire, 1999, *Communication Monographs, 66,* p. 113. Used by permission of the National Communication Association.

these results. Please refer to the section on multiple regression in Chapter 7 to get an understanding of what should be reported in the write-up of such an analysis. Then refer to the following examples for ideas on how to construct accompanying tables.

Table 8.12 is an example of how you might want to report a hierarchical regression analysis in tabular form:

TABLE 8.12   Hierarchical Regression Predicting Bulimic Action Tendencies ($N = 214$)

Predictor Variables	Zero-Order r	B	SE B	β	Block ΔR^2
Step 1 Demographics					.01
BMI	−.05	−.06	.02	−.03	
SES	−.02	−.02	.09	−.01	
Ethnicity	−.04	−.04	.08	−.04	
Age	−.09	−.05	.04	−.08	
Step 2 Endorse thin ideal	.30***	.45	.10	.30***	.09
Step 3 Total TV exposure	.01	.08	.03	−.002	.000
Step 4 Exposure to thin drama	−.11	−.14	.07	−.15*	.02
Step 5 Body image processing					.10
Question images	.22**	.10	.06	.12	
Compare images	.39***	.27	.08	.29**	
Images realistic and ideal	.24***	.06	.09	.05	
Step 6 Interactions					.04
Endorse × question		.23	.10	.17*	
Images real × question		−.26	.08	−.24**	
Endorse × TV drama		−.03	.12	−.02	
Endorse × total TV		.02	.06	.02	

Note. Total $R^2 = .21$. $F(14, 199) = 5.05$. $p < .001$. *$p < .05$, **$p < .01$, ***$p < .001$. From "Television Images and Adolescent Girls' Body Image Disturbance," by R. Botta, 1999, *Journal of Communication, 49,* p. 36. Used by permission of Oxford University Press.

The examples should give you some idea of the variety of ways that you can present your results in tabular form. Other examples of tables integrated with the text of a results section appear in the sections on many of the statistics in this book. Remember also to consult the section on the specific statistic for more information about what to report; all of the appropriate information for the results of your analysis need not appear in either a table or the text, but all of the information must appear somewhere in your results section.

Using Charts, Graphs, and Figures

> Design is choice. . . . Most principles of design should be greeted
> with some skepticism, for word authority can dominate our vision
> and we may come to see only through the lenses of word author-
> ity rather than with our own eyes. What is to be brought in designs
> for the display of information is the clear portrayal of complexity.
> Not the complication of the simple; rather, the task of the designer
> is to give visual access to the subtle and the difficult—that is, the
> revelation of the complex. (Tufte, 1983, p. 191)

Charts, graphs, and figures are much less common in published
social science research, mostly due to the fact that they are often
difficult to create and expensive to publish. However, these
means of presenting data in visual form can be extremely effective. Jacoby (1997) points out that "the statistical findings we report . . . provide the systematic evidence for our conclusions. But
how persuasive are those conclusions? To a great extent, it de-
pends upon how well we make the data speak. . . . [Y]ou need
also to show the data" (p. v). Presenting results in a visual form
can communicate the findings in a more elegant and persuasive
manner than words (or even tables) alone. Whereas tables are valued for their capacity to present precise values, figures—while
being less precise—excel in their capacity to convey structural
concepts inherent in the data. In other words, a good figure allows
readers to understand something important about the data or the
results at a glance.

We will use the term *figure* to mean anything that presents
data in a graphic form that is not a table. This includes pho-
tographs, line drawings, charts, and graphs. Once you have de-
cided that the data warrant the use of a figure (in spite of the cost
of its reproduction), the primary concern becomes one of quality.
The power of figures is easily lost if the figure cannot be produced
or reproduced well.

Although it is difficult to describe exactly how to create the
most appropriate figures to present your data, you should keep

some basic guidelines in mind. First, basic information from the data must be easily discernible. Cluttered graphs, or ones in which the data points are so tightly clustered as to be indistinguishable from one another, should be revised to make them more useful and easier to read.

Second, the layout of the figure should direct readers' attention toward what is important about the data, including interesting regularities and patterns of variation (Cleveland, 1993). By simply looking at the graph, a reader should be able to get a good idea of the relative magnitudes of each of the variables.

Third, because not all kinds of graphical information are understood by readers equally well, some kinds of graphs are better than others. The best graphs, according to Cleveland (1993), are those that show the difference between point locations. Elements that are harder for people to interpret are the differences in line length or in line angles (when these are representing the gist of the results).

There are some other, more technical, considerations to keep in mind when constructing a figure:

1. The data-to-ink ratio should be high; that is, the elements of the graph itself, including labels for axes and variables, should not heavily outweigh the presence of the data.

2. Graphics should tend toward the horizontal rather than the vertical.

3. Label the vertical axis so that the printing lies flat along the vertical axis. In other words, this label would be most naturally read if the reader were to turn the page sideways.

4. The effect (dependent variable) should be presented on the vertical axis; the cause (independent variable) should be presented on the horizontal axis. Axes should be clearly and simply labeled.

5. The typeface in the key or legend of the figure should be the same as the typeface used to label the axes, preferably a sans serif type such as Helvetica. Use upper- and lowercase letters to label the axes (title case), rather than all caps.

6. Be sure that the axes start at zero. If your units of measurement do not begin at zero, break the axis or axes with a double slash mark.

7. Any tick marks (lines used to indicate the levels of a variable along an axis) should point outward, not inward, from the scale lines. As few tick marks should be used as possible. This will facilitate reading of the figure.

Figures must also avoid two potential problems. First, figures should avoid misrepresenting the data by overlooking important features of the data. Presenting a portion of the data in such a way that invites false extrapolation does no good for a community of scholars trying to understand the significance of your study. Second, graphs should not impose patterns that do not really exist or that distort the true variability among observations.

Several different types of figures are commonly used in the social sciences. These include scatterplots, graphs and line graphs, and bar charts. A section on each of these types follows.

Bivariate Scatterplots

In addition to the guidelines discussed, some special guidelines are especially relevant for constructing scatterplots. First, the data rectangle should be slightly smaller than the scale rectangle. That is, no points of data should appear on the axis lines of your figure. Second, consider whether it is necessary to have rectangular grid lines. Scatterplots are sometimes easier to read without them. Third, transform data values so that they fill as much of the data rectangle as possible. A scatterplot constructed such that all of the data points form a mass in the center of the data rectangle is usually not as useful as one that avoids this problem.

Gutterbock (1997) constructed a very useful scatterplot to present the results of his study of *Money* magazine's report of the "Best Places to Live in America" (Figure 8.1).

Graphs and Line Graphs

Graphs (those that show absolute values and percentages) and line graphs (those that show the relationship between two variables) are probably the most common figures used in those social science journals that publish the results of quantitative studies. The exact contents of a line graph vary widely from journal to journal, but by adhering to the basic principles already outlined

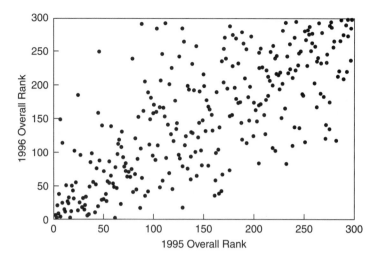

FIGURE 8.1   Interperiod Comparison of Rank for 298 Cities, 1995–96; $r = .74$

From Gutterbock (1997). *Public Opinion Quarterly, 61,* 342. Used by permission of the University of Chicago Press.

in this chapter, you should be able to create a useful and easy-to-understand line graph.

The following example in Figure 8.2 is taken from a study examining how long subjects took to fill out a personnel test. Holden (1998) asked one group of subjects to answer honestly and another group to lie on the test. He further divided the data into those who were honestly endorsing delinquent behavior and those lying in their endorsement as well as those who were honestly rejecting delinquent behavior and those who were lying when they said they rejected such behavior. Notice that the author provides means in parentheses next to the data points in the graph, and that the key is contained within the field of the graph.

This next example in Figure 8.3 also shows how a bivariate line graph can be used to convey the findings of a study. This example comes from a study on the effect of the mass media images on adolescent girls' bulimic behaviors (Botta, 1999). Note how the two figures are presented side-by-side in order to facilitate comparison between the two sets of findings.

Figure 8.4 makes the difference in men's and women's reactions to advertisements featuring "sexy" women clearer than a

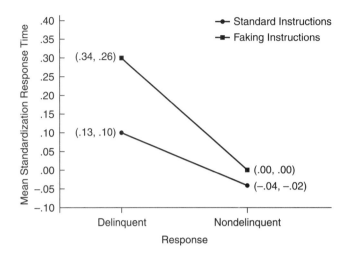

FIGURE 8.2   Mean Standardized Response Latencies as a Function of Faking Condition and Favorability of Response (means for responding true and false, respectively, are in parentheses)

From Holden, R. R. (1998). Detecting Fakers on a Personal Test: Response Latencies versus a Standard Validity Scale. *Journal of Social Behavior and Personality, 13*, 387–398.

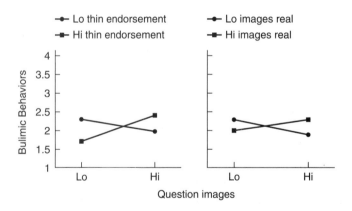

FIGURE 8.3   Means Estimate of Significant Regression Interactions for the Effect of Thin Endorsement on the Relationship between Question Media Images and Bulimic Behaviors and for the Effect of Seeing Media Images as Realistic Ideals on the Relationship between Question Media Images and Bulimic Behaviors

From Botta, R. (1999). Television images and adolescent girls' body image disturbance. *Journal of Communication, 49*, 22–41. Used by permission of Oxford University Press.

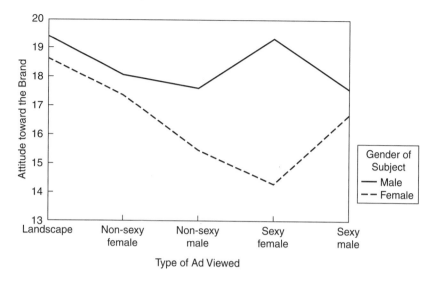

FIGURE 8.4   Attitude toward the Brand by Ad Type

From Jones, M. Y., Stanaland, A. J. S., & Gelb, B. D. (1998). Beefcake and Cheescake: Insights for Advertisers. *Journal of Advertising, 27*, 33–51. © Journal of Advertising.

table could have. The authors have placed the key outside of the field of the graph, perhaps because the lines in the graph vary enough that they do not have sufficient space for the key.

Bar Charts

Although bar charts are not as common as line graphs, they constitute another option for the visual display of your data. Bars are frequently used to show attributes of an independent variable that is categorical (such as gender or political affiliation). One of the principal challenges in developing bar graphs is creating comparisons between two or more groups by using bars that can be distinguished from each other. One of the bars is usually black, the other white; obtaining intermediate shades of gray is usually the biggest problem in producing a good bar chart.

The example in Figure 8.5 shows the degree to which Republican and Democratic activists changed their positions on the issue of abortion.

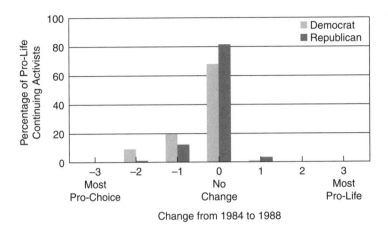

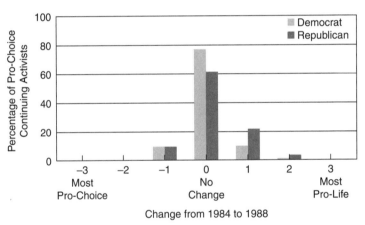

FIGURE 8.5   **Levels of Conversion on Abortion between 1984 and 1988 of Democratic and Republican Continuing Activists Who Took Pro-Life and Pro-Choice Positions in 1984**

From Layman & Carsey (1998). *Public Opinion Quarterly, 51,* 729. Used by permission of the University of Chicago Press.

Conclusion

When creating tables and figures, clarity should be your primary concern. If a figure does not contribute to readers' understanding in a way that cannot be gained through other means, it should be left out of a results section. The production expense that a figure entails will mean that journal editors will question whether it is truly necessary for readers to get a clear picture of your data or your results. However, there is no denying the power of presenting results in a visual format when done correctly. We hope that the guidelines presented in this chapter result in engaging, interesting, and effective tables and figures.

The fourth edition of the *Publication Manual of the American Psychological Association* (1994) provides excellent information and some examples of other types of figures not covered in this chapter, including dot maps and charts commonly used to illustrate path models. Because we do not cover how to write up results of these sorts of analyses, we have not included this type of figure. The APA manual also provides an excellent checklist for preparing figures for publication.

CHAPTER

9   Conclusion

Reporting statistics is a task that requires a balance between clarity and completeness. Results sections of manuscripts should provide enough information that knowledgeable scholars will be able to verify your interpretation of the data and get a detailed picture of the specifics of your findings. However, results sections need to be so clearly written that a reader with no knowledge of statistics should be able to understand what you found in your analysis.

Exactly what information needs to be reported in a results section in a manuscript is not usually controversial; yet few textbooks offer guidelines for which numbers need to be included in reports of statistical analyses. We have compiled information in this manual that can serve as a guideline for reporting the results of some of the most common statistical procedures. The ultimate format of your own results section will be determined by the design of your study.

Finally, this manual is not designed to replace any statistical manual; rather, we hope that this manual will supplement the book you usually reference for information about statistics. Other information about the details of the procedures for performing the test or other details about the statistic have not been provided as they are outside the scope of this text.

We hope that in the future, statistics texts will provide information about reporting each statistic (including examples) as a matter of course. Scholars begin as students, and we often retain our school texts for reference later in our careers. Statistical texts would be more helpful and complete with the incorporation of explanations and guidelines about the presentation of statistical results.

APPENDIX

Summary Chart of Statistics, What to Report, Abbreviations, and Suggested Syntax

Statistic	What to Report	Abbreviation	Suggested Syntax
Frequencies and Percentages	Size of overall data set	N	Respondents were recruited from communication courses ($N = 65$).
	Size of a cell or group	n	
	Percentages	%	
			Males represented a smaller proportion of the sample ($n = 25$) than women ($n = 40$).
			Of those participating in the study, only 35% were aware of the manipulation.
Mean and Standard Deviation	Mean	M	The mean of group one ($M = 3.25$, $SD = 1.12$) was greater than the mean of group two ($M = 2.45$; $SD = .99$).
	Dispersion measure	SD	
Cronbach's Alpha	Observed reliability coefficient	α (Cronbach's alpha)	$\alpha = .80$
			Cronbach's alpha = .80
	Descriptive statistics	M and SD	
Cohen's Kappa and Scott's Pi	Observed reliability coefficient	κ (Cohen's kappa)/π (Scott's pi)	$\kappa = .80$
			Cohen's kappa = .80
	Percentage of agreement		$\pi = .80$
	Number of items coded to establish reliability		Scott's pi = .80
	Number of coders		

Statistic	What to Report	Abbreviation	Suggested Syntax
Spearman Rank-Order Correlation	Degrees of freedom	df	r_s (df) = observed r_s value, significance level
	Observed r_s value	r_s	
	Significance level	p	
Pearson Product-Moment Correlation	Observed r value	r	r (df) = observed r value, significance level
	Significance level	p	
	Degrees of freedom	df	
	Descriptive statistics	M and SD	
Chi-Square Tests	Degrees of freedom	df	χ^2 (df, N = XX) = observed chi-square value, significance level, ES
	Number of observations	N	
	Observed chi-square value	χ^2	
	Significance level	p	
	Effect size	ES (varies with test)	
	Number of observations per cell	n	
	Table of frequencies / percentages	(optional)	
Wilcoxon Rank Sum Test/Mann-Whitney U Test	Observed z or U value	z/U	Group 1 (n = XX) was greater than Group 2 (n = XX), z [or U] = observed z [or U] value, significance level, ES
	Significance level	p	
	Effect size	ES (varies with test)	
	Number of observations	N	
	Number of observations per group	n	
	Mean ranks		
Kruskal-Wallis Test	Degrees of freedom	df	H (df, N = XX) = observed H value, significance level, ES
	Number of observations	N	
	Observed test value	H (or χ^2)	
	Significance level	p	
	Effect size	ES (varies with test)	
	Number of observations per group	n	
	Mean ranks		

Statistic	What to Report	Abbreviation	Suggested Syntax
McNemar's Repeated Measures Chi-Square Test for Change	Degrees of freedom	df	χ^2 (df, N = XXX) = observed chi-square value, significance level, ES
	Number of observations	N	
	Observed chi-square value	χ^2	
	Significance level	p	
	Effect size	ES (varies with test)	
	Number of observations per cell	n	
Cochran's Q	Degrees of freedom	df	Q (df, N = XX) = observed test value, significance level, ES
	Number of observations	N	
	Value of test statistic	Q (or χ^2)	
	Significance level	p	
	Effect size	ES (varies with test)	
	Number of observations per cell	n	
Wilcoxon Signed-Rank Test	Observed test value	T (or z)	N = XX, T = observed test value, significance level, ES
	Number of observations	N	
	Significance level	p	
	Effect size	ES (varies with test)	
	Rank sums (the number of +/'s)	SS	
	Descriptive statistics	M and SD	
Friedman Analysis of Variance by Ranks Test	Degrees of freedom	df	χ_r^2 (df, N = XX) = observed test value, significance level, ES
	Number of observations	N	
	Observed χ_r^2 value	χ_r^2 (or χ^2)	
	Significance level	p	
	Effect size	ES (varies with test)	
	Mean ranks		
	Number of observations per cell	n	

Statistic	What to Report	Abbreviation	Suggested Syntax
z Test	Degrees of freedom	df	z (df) = observed z value, significance level, ES
	Observed z value	z	
	Significance level	p	
	Effect size	ES (varies with test)	
	Number of observations	N	
	Sample mean and standard deviation	M and SD	
t Test	Degrees of freedom	df	t (df) = observed t value, significance level, ES
	Observed t value	t	
	Significance level	p	
	Effect size	ES (varies with test)	
	Number of observations	N	
	Number of observations per cell	n	
	Descriptive statistics	M and SD	
Analysis of Variance (ANOVA)	Degrees of freedom (between and within)	df_B/df_W	$F (df_B, df_W)$ = observed F value, significance level, ES
	Observed F value	F	
	Significance level	p	
	Effect size	ES (varies with test)	
	Number of observations	N	
	Number of observations per cell	n	
	Descriptive statistics	M and SD	
ANCOVA	What to report (in addition to ANOVA)		*For main effects and interactions:* $F (df_B, df_W)$ = observed F value, significance level, ES (accompanied by a table of adjusted group and cell means and standard deviations)
	Adjusted means	adj M	
	Covariate information (regression format)		

Statistic	What to Report	Abbreviation	Suggested Syntax
ANCOVA (continued)			*For covariate analyses:* F (df_B, df_W) = observed F value, significance level, partial ES (after covariates are removed). Accompanying table of pooled within-cell intercorrelations among the covariates and the dependent variable
MANOVA	Multivariate statistic	(varies) Wilks lambda, Pillais	Wilks lambda = observed λ value, F (df_B, df_W) = observed F value, significance level, ES
	Degrees of freedom (between and within)	df_B / df_W	
	Observed F value	F	
	Significance level	p	
	Effect size	ES (varies with test)	
	Univariate effects	(see ANOVA)	
	Number of observations	N	
	Number of observations per cell	n	
	Descriptive statistics	M and SD	
MANCOVA	What to report (in addition to MANOVA)		See ANCOVA
	Adjusted means	adj M	
	Covariate information (regression format)		
Regression and Multiple Regression	*Overall Model*		*For the model:* F (df_B, df_W) = observed F value, significance level, R^2, adj R^2 (accompanied by table with unstandardized regression coefficient, standardized regression coefficients)
	Multiple R	R	
	Effect size	R^2	
	Adjusted R^2	adj R^2	
	Observed F	F	
	Degrees of freedom	df	
	Significance level	p	

Statistic	What to Report	Abbreviation	Suggested Syntax
Regression *(continued)*	*Predictors*		*Individual relationships between the independent variables and dependent variables:* t = observed t value, significance level, effect size
	Unstandardized regression coefficient	B	
	Standardized regression coefficient	β	
	Observed t value	t	
	Significance level	p	
	Semipartial correlations	(variance accounted for per variable)	
Logistic Regression	*Overall Model*		R^2 = observed R^2 value, χ^2 (df, N = number of observations) = observed χ^2 value, significance level
	Observed χ^2 value	χ^2	
	Effect size	R^2	
	Degrees of freedom	df	
	Number of observations	N	
	Significance level	p	
	Classification results	(optional)	
	Predictors		
	Standardized regression coefficient	β	
	Observed Wald χ^2 value	χ^2	
	Significance level	p	
	Odds ratio		

REFERENCES

American Psychological Association. (1994). *Publication manual of the American Psychological Association* (4th ed.). Washington, DC: Author.

Andersen, P. A., Guerrero, L. K., Buller, D. B., & Jorgensen, P. F. (1998). An empirical comparison of three theories of nonverbal immediacy exchange. *Human Communication Research, 24* (4), 501–535.

Andsager, J. L., & Roe, K. (1999). Country music video in country's year of the woman. *Journal of Communication, 49,* 69–82.

Bahrick, L. E., Parker, J. F., Fishuv, R., & Levitt, M. (1998). The effects of stress on young children's memory for a natural disaster. *Journal of Experimental Psychology: Applied, 4* (4), 308–331.

Boster, F. J., Mitchell, M. M., Lapinski, M., Cooper, H., Orrego, V. O., & Reinke, R. (1999). The impact of guilt and type of compliance-gaining message on compliance. *Communication Monographs, 66,* 168–177.

Botta, R. (1999). Television images and adolescent girls' body image disturbance. *Journal of Communication, 49,* 22–41.

Brashers, D. E., & Jackson, S. (1999). Changing conceptions of "message effects": A 24-year overview. *Human Communication Research, 25* (4), 457–477.

Brock, D. M., Sarason, I. G., Sanghvi, H., & Gurung, R. A. R. (1998). The perceived acceptance scale: Development and validation. *Journal of Social and Personal Relationships, 15* (1), 5–21.

Burgoon, J. K., & LePoire, B. A. (1999). Nonverbal cues and interpersonal judgments: Participant and observer perceptions of intimacy, dominance, composure and formality. *Communication Monographs, 66,* 105–124.

Canary, D. J., Brossman, J. E., Brossman, B. G., & Weger, H., Jr. (1995). Toward a theory of minimally rational arguments: Analyses of episode-specific effects of argument structures. *Communication Monographs, 62* (3), 183–212.

Carletta, J., Garrod, S., & Fraser-Krauss, H. (1998). Placement of authority and communication patterns in workplace groups: The consequences for innovation. *Small Group Research, 29* (5), 531–559.

Carson, C. L., & Cupach, W. R. (2000). Facing corrections in the workplace: The influence of perceived face threat on the consequences of managerial reproaches. *Journal of Applied Communication Research, 28* (3), 215–234.

Cassara, C. (1998). U.S. newspaper coverage of human rights in Latin America, 1975–1982: Exploring President Carter's agenda-building influence. *Journalism and Mass Communication Quarterly, 75,* 478–486.

Chow, S. L. (1988). Significance test or effect size? *Psychological Bulletin, 103* (1), 105–110.

Cleveland, W. S. (1993). A model for studying display methods of statistical graphics. *Journal of Computational and Graphical Statistics, 2,* 323–343.

Cohen, J. (1965). Some statistical issues in psychological research. In B. B. Wolman (Ed.), *Handbook of clinical psychology* (pp. 95–121). New York: McGraw-Hill.

Collins-Jarvis, L. (1997). Participation and consensus in collective action organizations: The influence of interpersonal versus mass-mediated channels. *Journal of Applied Communication Research, 25* (1), 1–16.

Coombs, W. T., & Holladay, S. J. (1996). Communication and attributions in a crisis: An experimental study in crisis communication. *Journal of Public Relations Research, 8* (4), 279–295.

Cortina, J. M., & Dunlap, W. P. (1997). On the logic and purpose of significance testing. *Psychological Methods, 2* (2), 161–172.

Cozzarelli, C., & Karafa, J. A. (1998). Cultural estrangement and terror management theory. *Personality and Social Psychology Bulletin, 24* (3), 253–267.

DeSantis, A. (1998). Selling the American dream myth to black southerners: The *Chicago Defender* and the Great Migration of 1915–1919. *Western Journal of Communication, 62,* 474–511.

Engstrom, E., & Ferri, A. J. (1998). From barriers to challenges: Career perceptions of women TV news anchors. *Journalism and Mass Communication Quarterly, 75* (4), 789–802.

Fern, E. F., & Monroe, K. B. (1996). Effect-size estimates: Issues and problems in interpretation. *Journal of Consumer Research, 23* (September), 89–105.

Flamiano, D. (1998). The birth of a notion: Media coverage of contraception, 1915–1917. *Journalism and Mass Communication Quarterly, 75* (3), 560–571.

Ford, T. M., Liwag-McLamb, M. G., & Foley, L. A (1998). Perceptions of rape based on sex and sexual orientation of victim. *Journal of Social Behavior and Personality, 13* (2), 253–263.

Furnham, A., Meader, N., & McClelland, A. (1999). Factors affecting nonmedical participants' allocation of scarce medical resources. *Journal of Social Behavior and Personality, 13* (4), 735–746.

Furno-Lamude, D. (1994). Baby boomers' susceptibility to nostalgia. *Communication Reports, 7* (2), 130–135.

Gibson, R., & Zellman, D. (1998). Effects of citation in exemplifying testimony on issue perception. *Journalism and Mass Communication Quarterly, 75,* 167–176.

Gold, G. I., & Shaw, J. I. (1998). Causal chaining: The structure and complexity of accounts. *Journal of Social Behavior and Personality, 13,* 651–666.

Graetz, K. A., Boyle, E. S., Kimble, C. E., Thompson, P., & Garloch, J. L. (1998). Information sharing in face-to-face, teleconferencing, and electronic chat groups. *Small Group Research, 29* (6), 714–743.

Grewal, D., Marmorstein, H., & Sharma, A. (1996). Communicating price information through semantic cues: The moderating effects of situation and discount size. *Journal of Consumer Behavior, 23* (2), 148–155.

Grier, L. K., & Firestone, I. J. (1998). The effects of an intervention to advance moral reasoning and efficacy. *Child Study Journal, 28* (4), 267–285.

Gutterbock, T. M. (1997). Why *Money* magazine's "Best Places" keep changing. *Public Opinion Quarterly, 61,* 339–355.

Haynes, A. A., & Rhine, S. L. (1998). Attack politics in presidential nomination campaigns: An examination of the frequency and determinants of intermediated negative messages against opponents. *Political Research Quarterly, 51,* 691–721.

Hays, W. (1963). *Statistics for psychologists.* New York: Holt, Rinehart & Winston.

Hecht, M., Trost, M. R., Bator, R. J., & MacKinnon, D. (1997). Ethnicity and sex similarities and differences in drug resistance. *Journal of Applied Communication Research, 25* (2), 75–97.

Holden, R. R. (1998). Detecting fakers on a personnel test: Response latencies versus a standard validity scale. *Journal of Social Behavior and Personality, 13,* 387–398.

Honeycutt, J. M., Cantrill, J. G., Kelly, P., & Lambkin, D. (1998). How do I love thee? Let me consider my options: Cognition, verbal strategies, and the escalation of intimacy. *Human Communication Research, 25* (1), 39–63.

Hummert, M. L., Shaner, J. L., Garstka, T. A., & Henry, C. (1998). Communication with older adults: The influence of age stereotypes, context, and communicator age. *Human Communication Research, 25* (1), 124–151.

Inmann, M. L., Huerta, J., & Oh, S. (1998). Perceiving discrimination: The role of prototypes and norm violation. *Social Cognition, 16,* 418–450.

Jaccard, J., & Becker, M. A. (1997). *Statistics for the behavioral sciences* (3rd ed.). Pacific Grove, CA: Brooks/Cole.

Jacoby, W. G. (1997). *Statistical graphics for univariate and bivariate data.* Newbury Park, CA: Sage. (Michael Lewis-Beck, series editor).

Johnson, J. D., Meyer, M. E., Berkowitz, J. M., Ethington, C. T., & Miller, V. D. (1997). Testing two contrasting structural models of innovativeness in a contractual network. *Human Communication Research, 24,* 320–348.

Jones, M. Y., Stanaland, A. J. S., & Gelb, B. D. (1998). Beefcake and cheesecake: Insights for advertisers. *Journal of Advertising, 27,* 33–51.

Jordan, J. M. (1998). Executive cognitive control in communication: Extending plan-based theory. *Human Communication Research, 25* (1), 5–38.

King, C. M. (2000). Effects of humorous heroes and villains in violent action films. *Journal of Communication, 50* (1), 5–24.

Korsgaard, M. A., Roberson, L., & Rymph, R. D. (1998). What motivates fairness? The role of subordinate assertive behavior on managers' interactional fairness. *Journal of Applied Psychology, 83,* 731–744.

Kunkel, A. W., & Burleson, B. R. (1999). Assessing explanations for sex differences in emotional support: A test of the different cultures and skill specialization accounts. *Human Communication Research, 25,* 307–340.

Layman, G. C., & Carsey, T. M. (1998). Why do party activists convert? An analysis of individual-level change on the abortion issue. *Public Opinion Quarterly, 51,* 723–749.

Leach, M. S., & Braithwaite, D. O. (1996). A binding tie: Supportive communication of family kinkeepers. *Journal of Applied Communication Research, 24* (3), 200–216.

Leets, L., & Giles, H. (1997). Words as weapons—When do they wound? Investigations of harmful speech. *Human Communication Research, 24* (2), 260–301.

Lemert, J. B., Wanta, W., & Lee, T. T. (1999). Party identification and negative advertising in a U.S. Senate election. *Journal of Communication, 49* (2), 123–134.

LePoire, B. A., Burgoon, J. K., & Parrott, R. (1992). Status and privacy restoring communication in the workplace. *Applied Communication Research, 20* (4), 419–436.

Morgan, B. L. (1998). A three generational study of tomboy behavior. *Sex Roles, 39,* 787–800.

Morgan, S. E., & Reichert, T. (1999). The message is in the metaphor: Assessing the comprehension of metaphor in advertisements. *Journal of Advertising, 28* (4), 1–12.

Morrill, C., Johnson, M., & Harrison, T. (1998). Voice and context in simulated everyday legal discourse: The influence of sex differences and social ties. *Law and Society Review, 32,* 639–666.

Page, S. (1998). Accepting the gay person: Rental accommodation in the community. *Journal of Homosexuality, 36* (2), 31–37.

Pbert, L., Adams, A., Quirk, M., Hebert, J. R., Ockene, J. K., & Luippold, (1999). The patient exit interview as an assessment of physician-delivered smoking intervention: A validation study. *Health Psychology, 18* (2), 183–188.

Pfau, M., Kendall, K. E., Reichert, T., Hellweg, S. A., Lee, W., Tusing, K. J., & Prosise, T. O. (1997). Influence of communication during the distant phase of the 1996 Republican presidential primary campaign. *Journal of Communication, 47* (4), 6–26.

Pfau, M., Tusing, K. J., Koerner, A. F., Lee, W., Godbold, L. C., Penaloza, L. J., Yang, V. S., & Hong, Y. (1997). Enriching the inoculation construct: The role of critical components in the process of resistance. *Human Communication Research, 24* (2), 187–215.

Postmes, T., Branscombe, N. R., Spears, R., & Young, H. (1999). Comparative processes in personal and group judgments: Resolving the discrepancy. *Journal of Personality and Social Psychology, 76* (2), 320–338.

Potter, W. J., & Warren, R. (1998). Humor as camouflage of televised violence. *Journal of Communication, 48* (2), 40–57.

Reichert, T., Lambiase, J., Morgan, S., Carstarphen, M., & Zavoina, S. (1999). Cheesecake and beefcake: No matter how you slice it, sexual explicitness in advertising continues to increase. *Journalism and Mass Communication Quarterly, 76* (1), 7–20.

Rhee, J. W. (1997). Strategy and issue frames in election campaign coverage: A social cognitive account of framing effects. *Journal of Communication, 47* (3), 26–48.

Richardson, J. T. (1996). Measures of effect size. *Behavior Research Methods, Instruments, & Computers, 28* (1), 12–22.

Rimal, R. N., & Flora, J. A. (1998). Bidirectional familial influences in dietary behavior: Test of a model of campaign influences. *Human Communication Research, 24* (4), 610–637.

Robinson, J. D., & Skill, T. (1995). The invisible generation: Portrayals of the elderly on prime-time television. *Communication Reports, 8,* 111–119.

Roloff, M. E., & Janiszewski, C. A. (1989). Overcoming obstacles to interpersonal compliance: A principle of message construction. *Human Communication Research, 16,* 33–61.

Rosenthal, R. (1991). Meta-analytic procedures for social research. In L. Bickman & D. J. Rog (Eds.), *Applied Social Research Methods Series, Vol. 6.* Newbury Park, CA: Sage.

Rosenthal, R., & Rosnow, R. L. (1984). *Essentials of behavioral research: Methods and data analysis.* New York: McGraw-Hill.

Rosnow, R. L., & Rosenthal, R. (1996). Computing contrasts, effect sizes, and counternulls on other people's published data: General procedures for research consumers. *Psychological Methods, 1* (4), 331–340.

Rotenberg, K. J., Hewlett, M. G., & Siegwart, C. M. (1998). Principled moral reasoning and self-monitoring as predictors of jury functioning. *Basic and Applied Social Psychology, 20* (2), 167–173.

Rouet, J. F., Favart, M., Britt, M. A., & Perfetti, C. A. (1997). Studying and using multiple documents in history: Effects of discipline expertise. *Cognition and Instruction, 15* (1), 85–106.

Rudestam, K. E., & Newton, R. R. (1992). *Surviving your dissertation: A comprehensive guide to content and process.* Newbury Park, CA: Sage.

Sallot, L. M., Steinfatt, T. M., & Salwen, M. B. (1998). Journalists' and public relations practitioners' news values: Perceptions and cross-perceptions. *Journalism and Mass Communication Quarterly, 75* (2), 366–377.

Scandell, D. J. (1998). The personality correlates of public and private self-consciousness from a five-factor perspective. *Journal of Social Behavior and Personality, 13,* 579–592.

Seiter, J. S. (1997). Honest or deceitful? A study of persons' mental models for judging veracity. *Human Communication Research, 24* (2), 216–259.

Shontz, F. C. (1986). *Fundamentals of research in the behavioral sciences: Principles and practice.* Washington DC: American Psychiatric Press.

Siegel, S., & Castellan, N. J., Jr. (1988). *Nonparametric statistics for the behavioral sciences* (2nd ed.). New York: McGraw-Hill.

Simon, L., Greenberg, J., Arndt, J., Pyszczynski, T., Clement, R., & Solomon, S. (1997). Perceived consensus, uniqueness, and terror management: Compensatory responses to threats to inclusion and distinctiveness following mortality salience. *Personality and Social Psychology Bulletin, 23* (10), 1055–1065.

Solomon, D. H., & Williams, M. L. M. (1997). Perceptions of social-sexual communication at work: The effects of message, situation, and observer characteristics on judgments of sexual harassment. *Journal of Applied Communication Research, 25* (3), 196–216.

Stempel, G. H., & Westley, B. H. (1989). Presentation of research results. In G. H. Stempel & B. H. Westley (Eds.), *Research methods in mass communication* (2nd ed., pp. 388–403). Upper Saddle River, NJ: Prentice Hall.

Tabachnik, B. G., & Fidell, L. S. (1996). *Using multivariate statistics* (3rd ed.). New York: HarperCollins College Publishers.

Tufte, E. R. (1983). *The visual display of quantitative information.* Cheshire, CT: Graphics Press.

Valkenburg, P. M., & Beentjes, J. W. J. (1997). Children's creative imagination in responses to radio and television stories. *Journal of Communication, 47,* 21–38.

Wainer, H. (1997). Improving tabular display with NAEP tables as examples and inspiration. *Journal of Educational and Behavioral Statistics, 22* (1), 1–30.

Weiss, A. J., Imrich, D. J., & Wilson, B. J. (1993). Prior exposure to creatures from a horror film: Live versus photographic representations. *Human Communication Research, 20* (1), 41–66.

Weiss, A. J., & Wilson, B. J. (1998). Children's cognitive and emotional responses to the portrayal of negative emotions in family-formatted situation comedies. *Human Communication Research, 24* (4), 584–609.

Williams, F. (1979). *Reasoning with statistics* (2nd ed.). New York: Holt, Rinehart and Winston.

Wuensch, K. L., & Poteat, G. M. (1998). Evaluating the morality of animal research: Effects of ethical ideology, gender, and purpose. *Journal of Social Behavior and Personality, 13,* 139–150.

Wyer, N. A., Sherman, J. W., & Stroessner, S. J. (1998). The spontaneous suppression of racial stereotypes. *Social Cognition, 16* (3), 340–352.

AUTHOR INDEX

SUBJECT INDEX